TOP COP

'EMERGENCY MAN'
Some amazing experiences of Chief Inspector Gary
Raymond APM, OAM (Rtd)

Gary is affectionately known to his police mates as
'The Pink Panther'

BY DAVID R. NICHOLAS

Ark House Press
PO Box 1722, Port Orchard, WA 98366 USA
PO Box 1321, Mona Vale NSW 1660 Australia
PO Box 318 334, West Harbour, Auckland 0661 New Zealand
arkhousepress.com

Ark House Press, a division of Initiate Media.

ISBN: 978-0-9875839-5-6 (pbk.)

Cataloguing in Publication Data:
Title: Top Cop
ISBN: 978-0-9875839-5-6 (pbk.)
Subjects: Spiritual /Biography
Other Authors/Contributors: Nicholas, David

Cover design and layout by initiateagency.com

This book is dedicated to police officers who daily risk their lives to keep the rest of us safe.

ACKNOWLEDGEMENTS

A book is never the work of one person. Indeed while an authors' name may appear on the cover—the author is never alone. Many contribute in a multitude of ways. I think of words sent to me many years ago by Elisabeth Elliot the wife of Jim who was martyred. She said, "Tell it simply, tell it straight and see that it's true.' Neither this book nor any others I have written could have been written without the wise counsel of three friends who are no longer with us. Howard Crago, Roland Wolsely and Clifford Warne. These were incredible encouragers.

There are others far too numerous to mention who have been great encouragers. *Top Cop* came into being due to the openness and cooperation of Gary Raymond. There are of course those who have helped in many and varied ways in the production of this book... My thanks go to Linda Atkins, Stephen Mason, Karen Smith and in particular Joyce Poke. Joyce has an amazing eye for detail. My daughter Joanne has helped at various stages making sure the manuscript was ship shape and Bristol fashion. I must also add that it was Andrew Scipione who said, when we were discussing the book, 'Give God the glory.' That I have sought to accomplish. Readers will make their own judgement.

FOREWORD

A BRIEFING BY THE CURRENT COMMISSIONER
OF THE NEW SOUTH WALES POLICE FORCE
COMMISSIONER ANDREW SCIPIONE APM

The New South Wales Police Rescue Squad is the oldest, full-time, emergency rescue unit in Australia. Formed in 1942, the Rescue Squad was originally established as the "Cliff Rescue Squad" to retrieve injured people from cliff bases along the NSW coastline. Over the years, the role of the Squad expanded dramatically to take in community emergencies including bushfires, floods, and the rescue of trapped people in motor vehicle accidents, assisting other police in emergency duties, and organising searches for lost hikers.

In its 70 year history the NSW Police Rescue Squad has played important roles in a diverse range of rescues and emergencies across New South Wales and Australia. And throughout that proud history no other name has become quite synonymous with Police Rescue as Gary Raymond.

At the state's most extreme disasters and emergencies: the Granville Train Disaster, Thredbo Landslide, the Newcastle Earthquake, Luna Park Ghost Train Fire and the Hilton Hotel Bombing, Gary performed duty that would see him earn awards and be recognised in Australia and internationally for his bravery.

On the 14th of February 1972, Gary Ernest Raymond joined the NSW Police Force as a recruit. In the five years prior, Gary had been an ambulance officer.

Gary's first posting as a police officer was at Redfern Police Station, in the old Number 7 Division, performing general duties as a Probationary Constable.

Gary spent just over a year in that role before being chosen to join the elite NSW Police Rescue Squad. As a member of the Squad, Gary went on to perform over 1,500 rescues including 1,000 motor vehicle accident rescues, 200 vertical rescues, and 200 suicide crisis negotiation retrievals. He also attended searches, armed offender events, improvised explosive device situations, industrial rescues, domestic rescues and he performed duties as a rescue and observation crew member on the NSW police helicopter.

In the early 1980s Gary qualified as a designated detective. It was a change in career that would see him involved and in charge of many successful homicide and other criminal investigations including the tragic murder of nursing sister Anita Cobby at Blacktown and the murder of six year old Tess Debrincat at Quakers Hill.

In 1991 Gary was appointed as a senior investigator to the State's Royal Commission into Corruption in the Building Industry in New South Wales. Postings at Wetherill Park, Riverstone and Cabramatta followed before Gary was selected to command the Manly area for 3 years. During this time his rescue skills were again proven as he led the successful rescue of 500 passengers from a Manly ferry which ran aground at Little Manly Cove.

Chief Inspector Gary Raymond APM, OAM was a member of the NSW Police for 34 years. Prior to his retirement in December 2005, Gary was performing duty at the Blacktown Police Station as a duty officer specialising in emergency management and crime scene management.

Some of his many policing awards include the Police Commissioner's Olympic Citation for his policing, planning and operational management during the 2000 Olympic Games in Sydney; the Australian Police Medal (APM); the National Medal with Clasp; the New South Wales Police Medal for 34 years distinguished police service. He also has the Granville Train Disaster Medallion. On retirement Gary was awarded the Order of Australia Medal (OAM) and has been nominated for Australian of the Year in 2008 and 2012.

After retiring, Gary continues to present workshops to the community, churches and guest lectures at the NSW Police Rescue & Bomb Disposal Squad and Australian Federal Police.

Gary and his wife Michelle are both uniformed members of The Salvation Army at Parramatta.

Ecclesiastes 1:9 tells us that there is nothing new under the sun. Yet the life and career of Chief Inspector Gary Raymond APM, OAM (Rtd) comes as close to challenging that Bible passage as any man's could.

An ordinary man who made, and continues to make, an extraordinary contribution; his focus was on rescuing others until one day when he was rescued himself by Jesus Christ.

In the world of policing, there are many officers who have been called upon to save lives. Perhaps what sets Gary apart in that regard is the sheer number of lives he has saved pulling people back, quite literally, from the abyss?

However, many times Gary went further than simply saving a life. He often offered a path to a new life; born again in Christ.

Top Cop does more than tell the story of a committed and dedicated police officer and the amazing tales of people who, quite literally, owe their life to him. It is the story of a call to faith in all its forms. Faith in one's self; the rule of law; our police; and a higher power.

A P Scipione APM
Commissioner of Police
New South Wales Police Force

CONTENTS

Chapter One: **The Policeman's Work**　　　　1

- Dizzy Heights
- A Rubble Rescue
- The Slipping Hand
- Rescued from Oblivion
- The Policeman

Chapter Two: **And Deeds Most Deadly**　　　31

- The Suitcase Bomb
- Stamped and Dead
- In the Heat of the Moment
- How shall we tell them?
- Tess murdered at five
- Christmas Dinner with Tears

Chapter Three: **The Human Touch**　　　59

- Racket in the cell
- Vegemite Lifeline
- McDonald's Police Style
- To Forgive or Not to Forgive
- Human Shields
- Before the Man
- Drugs and Theology don't mix
- To lie or not to lie
- Night Nurses in a mess

Chapter Four: Angel Unaware   **83**

- Angel or Policeman
- Peter and the Train
- On knocking Teeth out
- Death in pajamas
- Stop at the Top

Chapter Five: All Creatures Great and Small   **103**

- Who doesn't know an Elephant?
- The Red Bellied Black Snake
- The Headless Dog
- The Swearing Cockatoo
- The Growling Doberman
- A Plea for Penguins
- On Stepping into a Fish Tank

Chapter Six: Matches on the Mind   **119**
- The Granville Train Wreck
- Raymond spends Ten hours rescuing two women
- The Risk of Explosion

Chapter Seven: Strange Ways of Normal (?) People **137**

- A Very Canny trick
- Bible Cigarettes
- On Catching Superman
- Moll Fire
- Too Hot to Handle
- Half a Million for a Dog

Chapter Eight: A Political Assassination   **147**

- A Political Assassination
- Raymond in Charge of the scene
- The Power of a speeding bullet

Chapter Nine: **The Shield of Faith**   155

•   Bold Testimony

Chapter Ten: **Risks Galore**   173

•   Gun at Chest
•   Good on You God
•   Wrestle in a Chemist shop
•   Vented Anger
•   The Meat Cleaver Man
•   Rifle in the back of a car
•   Murder Prevented

Chapter Eleven: **The Wrap Up And Tale Ender**   197

There are many other things that Gary did. One book alone could not even begin to contain the many adventures of Gary Raymond. It would take several books. At least this book will start to satisfy the demands of interested readers.

APPENDIX   199

•   Suicide Awareness and Prevention

CHAPTER ONE

THE POLICEMAN'S WORK

 ∽

"It's a dangerous business going out of your door."
J.R.R.Tolkien (Author)

"Dizzy Heights"

Gary Raymond was on duty at the Police Rescue Squad headquarters. A call came in. A man was trapped at the very top of one of Sydney's 100 metre high television transmission towers. Step by step, a young electrician had climbed his way up the steel tower via the ladders to repair an aerial for commercial radio use. The task took him some time and with trepidation. When he'd finished the job he packed up his tools. He was about to climb down, when for no apparent reason, he panicked, froze and had a serious anxiety attack. He then clung to the tower with all his might, not game enough to move or look down. Fortunately, he wore a harness. He stayed immobilised for about three hours unnoticed.

Information from bystanders told police that people in surrounding buildings, who'd been glancing out of their windows, finally realised the man hadn't moved. Observers were slow to react. They glanced at the man and went about their work. When they looked later the man still hadn't moved. Some thought he was 'bludging' on his boss or even sleeping on the job. Then finally someone said,

"I think something's wrong."

A call was made to 000,

"I don't want to panic the emergency services, but there's a man on the tower who's been there at least three hours and hasn't moved in a long time."

Even though this was the time before mobile phones, the man could not have used a phone because he was suffering from mental paralysis brought on by his 'panic attack'. He had no means of communicating with those below or around him even if he wanted to or could do. He wasn't capable of using a radio due to his distress.

The alarm went off at the Police Rescue Squad headquarters and along with his mates, Gary Raymond was on his way. When Gary arrived he used a pair of binoculars to check out the man at the top of the tower. By the look on the man's face, Gary knew he was alive and in trouble. He wasn't moving and he gripped the tower similarly to a monkey in the jungle gripping a tree. Gary put on his vertical rescue gear, strapped his portable radio to his waist and started the long climb to the top of the tower. Gary later discovered he couldn't hear his radio due to the wind noise at the top of the tower anyway. He took up a light rope which he would use to haul up a heavier rescue rope, slings and pulley block. It was very cold. Wind whistled around his body.

As Gary drew closer to the electrician there was a yell as the man looked at him, screamed and snapped, "Don't touch me, don't touch me, leave me alone, get away, leave me here."

At first Gary thought the man was suicidal. "I don't have a trapped worker, I have someone who wants to suicide" he thought.

This conclusion was reached because the man was as aggressive as suicidal people at heights are sometimes. In the past, people trapped at heights or depths had said to Gary,

"Thank God you're here. Please help me."

In this case the man said, "Get away, keep clear, I can't get down to the ground. Let me die here."

Gary told him not to look down. The sad part of the rescue was that the man would rather have died at the top of the tower rather than risk being lowered to the bottom with Gary. Worse than that, he had the attitude 'leave me alone, I'm going to die up here'. He was mentally locked up. Gary amusingly called it a 'brain drain'.

Gary said, "Come on mate I'm from the Police Rescue Squad, I've handled tower rescues before and done them successfully. I want to get you down. You will be safe with me. Trust me."

Without thinking, Gary was just about to tell the man to look down to verify his Police Rescue truck was present as a way of confirming who he was, but he quickly abandoned that idea realising it would make the situation worse. The last thing Gary wanted was the man to look down and increase his panic. After all, Gary had been telling him 'not to look down.'

Gary said, "I have our special harnesses here. I'd like to harness you and attach you to me; we'll then be lowered down in stages through the centre of the tower."

The man said loudly, "No, no, no. We'll fall. Let me die here, I'm not falling down there to die."

"No mate, we won't fall," Gary said calmly and decisively, "I will harness you to me and then we'll go down through the ladders together, the way you got here. I'll go first, and then you can follow me down the ladders."

The electrician now crying and breathing heavily said, "No, no, no, I'll fall. If you trip, I'll trip, we'll fall together; just leave me here, don't touch me!"

Gary realised this man couldn't think straight. He wasn't able to see his way out of the situation. Gary continued to talk to the man calmly, trying to be patient. He tried to reassure him that he could get him down from the tower not only alive, but uninjured. It was getting dark.

Gary said, "Look mate, the sun is going down. We don't want to be here in the dark".

Gary began to think this was going to turn into a 'marathon'. I can still get you down whether it's daylight or dark, but it would be easier and safer if we do it now while we've got daylight."

The man screamed, "No, just leave me here and get me when I die." He began to cry uncontrollably.

Gary realised the man actually did want to stay there and die. The electrician was in a sorry state.

Gary said with stern police authority in his voice, "Look mate, you are not staying here to die. That's not an option whether you like it or not. Now calm down and do what I tell you to do, understand that?"

He replied with a quivering voice, "Yes." Gary said, "I can harness you to me and we can be out of here very quickly and safely. Do you want to put the harness on or would you like me to put it on for you?"

The young electrician sensing Gary's assertiveness then agreed Gary could put the harness on. He had to let go one hand at a time but he had his hand wrapped around a girder and Gary had to literally squeeze the harness on past where he was squeezing his fingers onto the steel. His knuckles were white and you could just about see his protruding bones. The harness was finally on and the man was attached to Gary's harness. Gary had already set up a pulley block and rope above them which was controlled from the ground by his police rescue crew, police, firemen and ambulance officers.

Gary said, "I want you to let go now and you'll be quite safe. You're harnessed to me so we'll swing into the middle of the tower gently and we'll be lowered to the ground slowly okay?"

After what seemed an eternity for Gary, the man agreed yet every time they swung out to the centre of the tower, he would grab a girder with his hands. Gary patiently encouraged him to let go but each time they swung out, the man grabbed a girder again. Gary prized his fingers off only to have the other hand grab on. This continued to happen.

Finally in frustration Gary said, "Look mate, we can't keep going like this. You're making it difficult. I'm going to tie your hands behind your back with a bandage so that you can't grab the girders."

"No, no, no," he yelled. "Please don't do that."

Without permission, Gary tied the man's hands behind his back with a bandage. This was very difficult. First Gary held the man's thumbs together behind the back. Next he tied a bandage around the wrists.

Gary thought, "I wish I had my handcuffs."

Unfortunately, these had been left in the rescue truck safe box because the electrician after all wasn't a criminal. To make matters worse the man shook violently, either because he cold, scared or maybe both. Finally, Gary got the man to agree to descend. By this time he was not just screaming, but 'shrieking' at the top of his voice. Gary's ears were ringing as he crunched up his face with discomfort. Gary realised the one thing he'd never put in his vertical rescue kit, was a set of ear plugs! He certainly put some in after this job! They started to descend. The man suddenly lashed out with his legs and managed to get his legs around one of the upper steel cross girders. He hung on for dear life. At one stage the pair nearly turned upside down before Gary stopped the decent with his whistle signal.

Gary said loudly, "Don't do this mate. You're harnessed, you're safe. Just trust me and let's get down out of here right now."

To Gary's utter amazement, he still hung on to the girder with his legs. Like the hands earlier, as Gary prized one foot off, the man used his other foot to try and grab a hold. The man was panting and crying in panic.

Gary pleaded and said, "Mate, I'm going to tie your ankles up now. I'm going to wrap your legs up so that you can't grab the girders."

"Yes, but I know I'm going to die. I'm going to fall," he said whimpering.

Gary was exasperated and said, "How can you fall when you're all tied up and linked to me?" "Now wake up to yourself and stop this nonsense", Gary said with stern voice finally losing his patience.

After being raised back to the top, Gary wrapped the bandage around the fellow's hips and all the way down to his ankles. By the time he'd finished the man looked like a mermaid or half an Egyptian mummy! Gary had a good laugh to himself, keeping a straight face of course. This rescue was done with great difficulty but with an amusing side. They started to descend again. This was done through a series of pulley blocks by the team on the ground letting the rope out hand over hand. Because of the wind, Gary used a referee's whistle. This allowed him to communicate with his mates on the ground. The bosses on the ground were the late Sergeant Ray Tyson and the late Sergeant Bill Fahey who were both like a father to Gary with the other young blokes in the squad as well. Gary knew he was always safe with Ray and Bill in charge. The whistle signals were vital when police portable radios wouldn't work due to the wind blowing into the microphone or maybe bad reception. Wind conditions, surrounding noise or bad reception often distorted voices on the radio.

Whistle signals were reasonably simple and used often by Police Rescue on vertical rescues successfully in all conditions.

One long blast meant down.

One short blast meant stop.

Two blasts meant up.

A series of quick short blasts meant crisis or trouble.

All the way down the electrician screamed. Keep in mind he was right next to and facing Gary in the harness. Having used bandages, the only thing Gary needed was a sock to stuff into the guy's mouth to shut him up. But that was not allowed Gary told me, with a smile. Police brutality! As their feet touched the ground the man fainted. The ordeal had been too much. As he hung off Gary's harness, other members of the rescue team came forward and released the man. Gary, with his ears still ringing, was free at last after what had seemed ages being hooked up to a man who didn't want to be rescued. Finally, Gary's ears could recover.

Sergeant Tyson said to Gary, "We thought you were going to spend the night up there boy."

"So did I Ray for a minute or two," Gary said angrily.

"Next time I'll take a cut lunch."

Sergeant Fahey sarcastically but jokingly said, "That will be the day you'd take sandwiches. It would be more like garlic prawns for you."

He knew Gary loves seafood. Gary, still annoyed with the electrician's extremely difficult rescue, ignored them as laughter broke out. The man was carried to a nearby ambulance.

Gary was packing his gear away when a paramedic approached him and said, "Your mate from the tower wants to see you before we leave."

"How's he doing?"

"He's fine. A blithering mess mentally but he's alright physically. He's a little hypothermic due to the cold and he's still crying his eyes out. He keeps shaking his head and says he thought he was going to die either at the top of the tower or splattered on the concrete below."

Gary shook his head and sniggered.

Gary walked over to the rescued electrician and sat beside him on the back step of the ambulance. The man had a blanket or two wrapped around him; they'd been giving him some oxygen to get him going.

Gary said, "You wanted to see me mate. How are you feeling?"

"I'm pretty lucky to be alive. I really thought I was going to die up there or die down here."

Gary replied, "You were pretty panicky up there mate. What happened?"

He said, "I've done a couple of tower jobs but I'm fairly new at the game. This is the biggest tower I've ever climbed. I really don't know what happened. I work alone and I know now I should have had someone with me, but I need the money. I just snapped and couldn't move. I'm sorry for all the trouble I've caused you."

"That's okay mate, you were scared, I understand. It's a healthy 'fear of heights' that keeps us alive in the rescue squad."

The rescued man replied, "No, I'm sorry because I didn't trust you. You told me I could trust you and that you'd get me down safely. You're an experienced officer from the Police Rescue Squad. You're used to heights. You told me you'd climbed cliffs, towers, ladders and buildings many times before. I didn't believe you could get me down safely. I failed to trust you."

"I understand mate but in the end, you trusted me enough to allow me to bandage you up and bring you down."

The man cried again and said, "I still didn't trust you. I really thought I was going to die. I want to apologise. Can you forgive me?

I now know you are completely trustworthy and you saved me. You knew what you were doing. What you promised to do, you did. At the time I didn't see it. I should have, but I didn't. I'm sorry."

Gary replied, "Hey, that's okay mate. Just because you didn't trust me, didn't mean I wasn't going rescue you? I didn't say, "Well, if you don't trust me you can stay here and die. I'm leaving. I went on talking with you to try and get you to trust me enough so that I could get you down, which of course we did. No need to apologise, I understand, just settle down and recover, you're safe now. Catch you later."

Gary shook his cold quivering hand. It was a strong grip by the man who didn't let go for a few seconds more than the normal handshake. He was so grateful for Gary 'saving his life' although to Gary, it was just another rescue job. Gary then climbed back up the tower and gathered up his lowering equipment. He went back to base for a well earned rest if possible before the next rescue call.

Shrugging his shoulders, Gary told me, "That's what they pay me to do."

When thinking about this incident later, Gary's Salvation Army background came to the fore.

He told me, "God is not a liar. Sometimes, people don't believe the Lord Jesus Christ will do what He says He will do in His word, the Bible, to rescue us for eternity. We don't trust the Lord fully. We disregard Him, judge Him or blame Him for the mess we've created in the world ourselves. Fear or complacency overtakes us when we don't trust Him." The man on the tower proved the point for Gary. It was all a matter of trust. The Lord God promises to forgive and save us if we turn away from our sin to Him. Just trust Him in all situations. He is the ultimate rescuer. He surely will achieve our rescue both here and into eternity if we trust Him to do that. Confession of our sin and repentance means apologising to God for not trusting Him in all circumstances. We then turn away from our sin and unbelief to Him. We continue to thank Him for loving us despite our mistrust in Him sometimes. Just do what He says in His word. Yes, He is trustworthy."

"A Rubble Rescue"

The word 'rescue' can have several meanings for Gary Raymond. Rescue who or what? None could have been stranger with coincidence than one that happened one weekend when Gary was on duty as an ambulance officer. Gary had a mate who worked in the demolition industry. He asked him if he had anything planned for Saturday night? Since they were both working n Saturday, they agreed to go out after work. Gary's mate didn't say where he was working, but Gary was working at NSW Ambulance Headquarters in Quay Street, Sydney. They arranged to meet at his mate's place around 6 o'clock that evening to have a night out.

About the middle of that Saturday morning, Gary was in the meal room when the emergency phone rang.

A voice from the Control Room said, "We have a casualty call for you, it's a call to a demolition site in Abercrombie Street, Chippendale. The side wall of a building has collapsed and someone is trapped and injured. The Police Rescue Squad is on the way."

Gary went down to the site siren blazing and red light revolving. There were people everywhere near a big pile of bricks, timber and debris. The crowd, including demolition workers, pointed to the rubble. A worker was covered in bricks and dust. Fortunately, he'd fallen across a flooring beam. This prevented him falling further into the basement. He straddled the beam. When Gary reached him he saw that only his neck and head were exposed. Police Rescue was on the way. He noticed the worker had quite a few bruises and abrasions. As Gary worked on the man he carefully cleared away the dust from around his mouth, face, eyes and head. After doing this Gary placed an oxygen therapy mask on the man's face. Next he placed a cervical collar around his neck just in case there was a spinal injury.

As Gary knelt on the debris he said, "Can you hear me mate?"
He said, "Yes."
Gary asked, "Were you knocked unconscious?"
He said, "I think I was for a short time."

Gary said, "Have you got any pain anywhere?" There was no reply.

Gary asked, "What's your name?"

To his surprise Gary got this reply, "You should know Gazza."

Gary said, "Do you know me?"

"Yes you idiot, it's Paul."

Gary was shocked to the core, "What are you doing here mate, what happened?"

He said, "I told you I would be working today, this is the site. The wall collapsed. I was on top of it."

Gary replied, "Wow, I don't believe it's you. Stay calm mate we'll have you out as quickly as possible."

Gary told me that when emergency workers attend the scenes where people they know are killed or injured, it takes on special significance. You become personally attached whereas other scenes you are able to detach as you don't know them. Paul was covered in dust and normally wore glasses. These had been knocked off in the fall. All of this made it hard for Gary to recognise his mate. What a huge surprise. Gary then recalled that they had discussed the fact they would both be working on Saturday. They had planned a night out after work. As they cleared the debris away Paul was released by police rescue, his injuries treated by Gary. This took about 45 minutes. They then removed Paul from the debris. He was sore and uncomfortable. Not only did he fall, but debris fell on top of him as well. Gary immobilised Paul's spine and he was lifted onto a stretcher and then taken in Gary's ambulance to the Royal Prince Alfred Hospital for assessment and treatment. On the way Gary sat in the rear of the ambulance continually checking Paul's condition. Paul asked Gary if he'd let his girlfriend know what had happened.

Gary said, "How am I going to tell her without sending her into a panic?"

Paul replied, "That's now your problem."

Gary finished work about 5 o'clock and went to Paul's girlfriend's place.

When he knocked on the door she said, "Hi Sue. It's Gary here."

She said, "Paul's not back from work yet. You blokes are having a boy's night out aren't you?"

Gary said, "Yes we were, but our plans have changed. I'm going home and Paul will be spending the night with a few nurses."

Surprised with bulging eyes she growled, "He'd better not, otherwise I'll kill him." Gary said, "Oh yes, I saw him today. I dropped around to where he was demolishing an old hotel in Abercrombie Street and ended up taking him to hospital."

"Why?" she answered confused.

Gary putting his hand up to calm her, replied gently, "He ended up bruised and battered from a wall falling."

She said, "What do you mean?"

Gary said, "I got a call to a demolition site and found Paul trapped and injured." Gary quickly added, "Paul's just fine and in a satisfactory condition. Come on Sue get ready, I'll take you to the hospital to see him." Needless to say, the boy's night out was postponed.

Paul did in fact spend the night with some nurses, without the wrath of his girlfriend. He was discharged after three days, none the worse for wear. Paul's girlfriend is one lady who will never forget the way Gary Raymond broke the news to her. With bad news, always just tell it gently, a little bit at a time." Gary told me Paul and his girlfriend eventually broke up. It was nothing to do with him with the nurses.

"The Slipping Hand"

It was a wet Saturday night when an urgent call came to the Police Rescue Squad. They were needed at the Sydney Harbour Bridge where a man was in trouble.

When Gary and his mates arrived, a detective ran up to Gary and said, "Quick Gaz. Hurry up otherwise we'll lose him." They hurried towards the bridge railing on the eastern side.

Gary anxiously asked, "What have we got?"

"Quick I'll show you," said a just as anxious detective.

They ran across to the eastern side of the bridge. Police had stopped the traffic. To his horror, Gary saw a man hanging over the side of bridge held by a single police handcuff around his wrist. Yes, just one handcuff!

Gary quickly asked, "How did this happen?"

"The bloke climbed over the top of the barbed wire fence onto the outside of the bridge and threatened to jump. I grabbed him through the gap under the fence, handcuffed one of his wrists, and then clicked the other handcuff onto the bridge. He tried to get away from me. In his haste he slipped on the wet steel on which he was standing and ended up hanging there over the water by the wrist on a single handcuff."

In telling me about the incident, Gary said the man was 'squealing' like a baby piglet. Looking at the man's hand Gary noticed the skin above the handcuff was swollen and slowly slipping. He knew his hand would soon 'de-glove' and draw blood if his weight wasn't urgently supported. Without doubt, he would fall and crash into the water of Sydney Harbour minus the skin on that hand. Gary ran back to the rescue truck for a ladder, hessian bag and two harnesses. He hurriedly put the ladder up against the barbed wire and covered it with bags. He climbed up the ladder, over the wire and down the outside of the bridge beside the man one hundred metres above the water.

In between his squeals the man cried, "My hand hurts, don't let me fall, please save me!"

Gary thought it a strange comment from a man who was threatening to jump. Gary placed a harness on the man and passed a rope through a gap allowing other police to take the man's weight. The handcuff on the bridge was unlocked by Gary. The man was lifted back over the fence onto the bridge where ambulance officers treated him before taking him to hospital. Reflecting on this incident, Gary believes the man had only seconds before the hand, stripped of skin, would have caused him to slip and plunge into the murky waters of Sydney Harbour and probably to his death. Because of the slippery condition at the time, the detective had virtually saved the man's life by handcuffing him to the bridge and then Gary placed the harness on just in time. His hand required extensive surgery and he was later taken to a mental health facility for support.

"He kept his life but lost some skin", Gary said.

"Rescued from Oblivion"

Not everyone can claim they've been saved from a murder plot twice. Such is the case of Gary Raymond. The same person came close to murdering Gary on two separate occasions. That person was his own mother! As Edward Fitzgerald put it, "The moving finger writes, and having writ, moves on nor all thy piety nor wit shall lure it back to cancel half a line, nor all thy tears wash out a word of it." We often wonder what might have been, 'if.' In the case of Gary Raymond he nearly wasn't (twice over!) But now with strong faith Gary can say along with the prophet Jeremiah, "Before I formed you in the womb I knew you: Before you were born I sanctified you." *(The Bible, Jeremiah 1:5)*

Gary's parents Jack Peel Raymond and Beryl Joan Harris met in 1948. Jack was a returned soldier and Beryl, a process worker. In 1950, they went to a dance together at Stockton near Newcastle in New South Wales. Later that night, in a moment of passion, Gary was conceived on Stockton Beach. When Beryl Harris found out she was pregnant, it put her in utter turmoil. As a result, she had a real battle knowing what to do. The unthinkable had happened. In her fear and embarrassment of people finding out, she considered terminating this unwanted child. Whichever way she looked at it, she'd be responsible for killing the child yet unborn to time. But that didn't matter at that time. It was all about her. The only option she thought was to not tell a soul, to have an abortion and keep it all quiet. Distressed, she finally decided to have her baby terminated. She didn't even tell Jack fearing he might reject her.

She booked into a women's clinic in a back street at Cooks Hill. She didn't go to work that day and obtained a loan from her bank manager. She lied to him saying the money was to buy a new bicycle to get to work, however it was to fund the abortion. At the clinic Beryl saw four women in the waiting room. Two chatted as they glanced at magazines. One woman stared at the floor, another was a fast knitter. The click, click of the knitting needles drove Beryl mad but she kept her cool as she thought about her own pregnancy and what would happen if anyone found out. She looked out of the window to make sure no one saw she was there. Years later, Beryl told Gary that as she looked around the room, she wondered why each woman was there.

"What circumstances lead each woman to this? Circumstances like mine?"

Deep in her thoughts, she speculated as to what this baby she was about to get rid of might turn out like? Was it a boy or girl? What would it look like? What would it have done if allowed to live?' Enormous fear of people finding out, especially her mother, drove Beryl to stick with her decision at that time.

Beryl told Gary the clinic was a big old terrace house, high ceilings and timber floors, with no heating or cooling. Every sound echoed from each room. A handwritten list of women's names was pinned straight onto on the waiting room wall. The list included Miss Beryl Harris. She told Gary she was third on the list. Beryl sat and waited her turn. Her heart pounded and her mouth was dry. A grossly overweight middle aged nurse in uniform walked from room to room getting organised for the day's work. She looked unhappy and was ignoring the patients. That nurse terrified Beryl.

At one stage 'the grump' looked at the four women and said as she huffed and puffed her words, "You'll be here most of the day under observation ladies after your procedure, so make sure you go to the toilet before I call you in. There's one out the back. We'll have enough mess without your business going everywhere as well."

Beryl was stunned. She was going to be a mess in more ways than one.

The doctor, an elderly man, arrived and chirped, "Good morning" to the receptionist and nodded to the four women, but didn't eyeball them.

The two women before Beryl were called in. At one stage she heard crying which made her anxious, however it was deathly quiet most of the time. She heard what sounded like instruments being dropped into a metal tray and a metal bucket or something else being put on the wooden floor. When each woman went in, the nurse deliberately crossed their name off the list on the wall.

Finally, the nurse came out, looked at the list and spoke with a loud authoritarian voice, "Miss Beryl Harris, Miss Harris."

Beryl stood up, looked through the open door of the procedure room and saw medical staff in green gowns and masks. She remembers seeing the eyes of who she thought was the doctor peering over his surgical mask. That frightened her as they were so 'cold' looking almost like the devil himself, she told Gary. It felt like her heart skipped a beat. She trembled and wanted to cry, but held back. The nurse had stressed the 'Miss' part of Beryl's name just to rub in the fact she was pregnant out of wedlock. Beryl told Gary, a deep feeling came over her not to destroy her baby. She realised later, it was God. The feeling caused her to leave the room and run down the road away from the clinic. She didn't even ask for her money back. No matter what the result, she now could not destroy her and Jack's baby. She loved Jack and would have to 'cop' the flack from her mother at home. She also feared that her mother would reject Jack and attempt to prevent their relationship.

Tears streamed down her face as she ran towards home. She was alone, vulnerable and scared. Several times she stopped to avoid people who might see her in tears. She reached a park, sat on the grass behind a hedge away from public seating in case she saw someone who knew her. It dawned on her, she'd have to face her mother and stepfather sooner or later and tell them she was pregnant. She was out of wedlock. She was a 'Miss' not a 'Mrs,' a serious embarrassment for a family in those days, unlike most today. Beryl agonised with fear. She knew the distress it would cause her mother. She wondered whether she should have gone back to the clinic.

Her family had migrated from England after her father died. They were a proud and a well respected middle class family. In those days, to have a pregnant daughter out of wedlock was not a good thing either morally, socially or financially. Beryl had a good job which was another worry. Would she get the sack? By the time she ran and walked, Beryl was home in time for the evening meal. When she entered the house she shut herself in her bedroom. Later that evening, she told her mother and stepfather what had happened. Beryl told Gary it was as if the whole house shook. Her mother was distraught but her stepfather stayed calm. After the dust settled, she talked things over with her mother. It was discussed as to whether Beryl should go to the country, have the baby and have it adopted out without anyone knowing. Her mother would tell people Beryl was working in the country for experience.

Finally, it was decided she should find Jack Raymond, the father of this baby as soon as possible and see if he would marry her. The quicker the better to avoid the possibility this may be found out by family, friends and neighbours. Beryl searched for Jack. She found him at the New Lambton Hotel drinking and singing with his mates. Beryl told Gary, she stood at the door until Jack noticed her and came out.

When she finally told him she was carrying his baby, he said calmly without delay, "Well Beryl, I'll marry you to give our child its mum and dad."

He could have said he wasn't ready for marriage, but made no excuses. As a former Australian Army soldier who served overseas during World War 2, he was a man of honour and would never shirk his responsibility. Jack Raymond had a good upbringing even though they were a poor family having lost his father due to tuberculosis when Jack was young. Gary told me his father's willingness to immediately commit to marry his mother touches his heart with pride in his dad, even today. He loved Beryl. The result was to prepare a 'shotgun wedding'. This was quickly arranged to occur in two weeks. The two were married. Gary's mother wasn't allowed to wear a white dress as she was not a 'virgin'. She wore a pale blue dress with a touch of white instead. Beryl says it was a kind of punishment or badge of dishonour in those days for being pregnant out of wedlock.

"People must have worked it out for themselves given the urgency of the marriage there was probably no doubt I was expecting", Beryl said to Gary.

On hearing the news from Beryl, Jack was too scared to tell his mother or even visit Beryl's mother and stepfather.

Aunty Shirley told Gary that on the day of the wedding, Jack said to his mother,

"Get ready Mum. We're going to a wedding this afternoon."

Nanna asked, "Whose wedding Jack?"

He said, "Mine mum."

Nanna Raymond panicked, not because of the sudden wedding notification, but because her only decent 'going out' dress was soaking wet on the clothesline. It was hurriedly removed, ironed dry by Aunty Shirley and made ready for the wedding.

On 20 May 1950, Jack aged twenty four, and Beryl aged twenty were married.

At 4.05am on Wednesday 13 December 1950, Gary Ernest Raymond was born. Jack was not at the hospital but away playing cricket. He arrived later. Men didn't watch the birth of their child in those days. It was a woman's business. He loved his cricket with the Water Board team and the mate's drink after the game couldn't be missed. Gary was born with a 'hair lip' which shocked his mother.

Aunty Shirley told Gary, "Everyone felt sorry for you and called you a poor little fella with the hair lip."

Gary's mother needed a great deal of assurance during Gary's hair lip surgery. Gary's mother told him that she first thought it was a 'curse' from God to remind her of becoming pregnant without being married. She soon changed that view and Gary's lip surgery was successful.

After Gary, four brothers were born over the next eight years, Neil, Kevin, Trevor and Brian. Gary's mother told him she was trying to have a girl after him. She gave up after giving birth to four other boys fearing she would have more boys if they kept trying. It could have been a cricket or football team. Interesting to note Gary, Neil and Kevin all became police officers. Trevor became a mechanical engineer, Brian an electrician and TAFE college teacher. Gary said he deeply loves his brothers (all good mates), all of his family and extended family. They get along well standing by each other in good times and bad. Amazingly, Gary, Neil and Kevin all attended the Granville Train Disaster on 18th January 1977. Gary was in Police Rescue, Neil in Disaster Victim Identification and Kevin in General Duties. Gary and Neil also attended the Hilton Hotel Bombing on 13th February 1978.

Life for Gary's parents and brothers was not easy due to his Dad's low wage as a storeman at the Electric Light Company in Georgetown. They all lived with Jack's mother, Nanna Raymond in her house in Thalaba Road, New Lambton. Space was a premium. It was a small three bedroom weatherboard tin roofed house supported on concrete pillars built in the early 1900's. An old coal fireplace provided winter warmth using Nanna Raymond's free coal allowance as an aged pensioner from the Local Council. During the summer, a cool southerly breeze journeyed through the front door, down the hallway and out the back door on most evenings. Gary called it nature's air conditioning. There was an outdoor toilet until renovations after the Newcastle earthquake when an inside toilet was built. There was no shower, just a big bath which was filled with hot water from a gas heated copper. Bath time for the entire family was often in the same water. If you were fortunate, you got an extra bucket top up as the bath water cooled off. The copper also provided a clothes washing container with an old timber 'T' type clothesline which stretched the length of the backyard. The copper full of hot water was even used to pluck and gut freshly killed chickens for Christmas.

Overcrowding was a factor. There were eight people in the house including six males with lots of dirty clothes and mouths to feed. It was a small kitchen/dining room and extra bedroom. Other family members also stayed there from time to time. Living this way was not easy for Nanna Raymond or Gary's mother. It caused friction and many upsets with two ladies in the same kitchen. No arguments, just brooding and getting into each others way. Without ever owning a car, the Raymond family had to travel by foot, bus, bicycle or train.

Sometimes they went in a neighbour's car. It was stressful, since outings or travel were not only expensive for the limited budget, but time consuming and uncomfortable, especially in bad weather. Gary and his brothers made their own fun at home, around neighbouring streets, beach, bushland; former coal mines shafts, storm water drains or swamps.

Gary jokingly told me, "It's a wonder we weren't all killed by the things we got up to. Mum and dad never knew half of it. As adults, we told them what we got up to and they didn't believe us. "

Gary's mum worked part time as a waitress and cleaner to make ends meet. She'd also bring home 'leftovers' from catering jobs to give the family some treats. It was like Christmas to get things to eat that they would not normally afford like professional cakes, pies and sausage rolls. Over time, she became depressed and angry through sheer fatigue and working long hours. She desperately wanted her own home but couldn't afford it. Jack was never physically abusive, but they yelled and argued about money and living conditions. Both parents sometimes lost it and swore at each other and the boys. When he was drunk, Gary's father was very sarcastic.

He'd berate Gary by saying things like, "You'll never have to do what I did in the war."

They found out later Jack suffered Post Traumatic Stress Disorder after the war like so many others. The three eldest boys had one room and the two youngest, in the other. Nanna had her own bedroom and went from her house on regular occasions to stay with Gary's late Aunty Shirley and Uncle John at Glendale. They were kind people. This gave some relief to the tension both felt living together. Gary's mother told him that she loved Nanna however; the pressure of having two women living in a packed house would take its toll.

Gary's father became a soldier in the Australian Army and trained at Canungra in Queensland. This was a jungle warfare training camp. It was tough training. When war broke out in 1939, the Australian Army's equipment was of WW1 vintage condition. Worse still, the army didn't have any doctrine for jungle warfare prior to 1942.

General Blamey decided to establish jungle training and as a result, a camp was opened at Canungra, Queensland. This is where Gary's father did his jungle warfare training. The training was extremely tough, but Jack did well.

The training at Canungra was so thorough it was said, "Soldiers trained there reacted with almost miraculous quickness to conditions in jungle warfare."

No wonder Jack Raymond often talked about how hard the training was.

He told his family, "A lot of blokes took off 'Absent without Leave' as they couldn't cope with it. When a train of new recruits came in, you'd shut your mouth about how tough the camp was, otherwise you would have to stay in camp and do the training all over again. No way had any of us wanted to do that again."

Jack was also stationed at Cowra and was present when Japanese prisoners broke out of the camp. He never forgot the time when a young Australian Army officer, Lieutenant Harry Doncaster, was killed when ambushed during the recapture of the Japanese prisoners. That is, the ones who didn't suicide or kill each other to avoid capture. The lieutenant was discovered dead with his head squashed in using a rock by an escaped Japanese prisoner. There was much tension at the camp when the soldiers, including Jack, had their .303 military rifles taken from them leaving only the bayonet to defend themselves. This was done in case escaped Japanese prisoners overwhelmed the soldiers and got hold of the Australian's rifles during the hunt to recapture them.

After Cowra, Jack was sent to the jungles of Papua New Guinea. Whilst trekking through the jungles of New Guinea, Jack looked over at another Australian Army unit going in the opposite direction. In utter amazement, through the dense jungle vegetation, he saw his brother Bill Raymond. Bill later fought on the Kokoda Tail and joined the NSW Police Force after the war. They broke ranks, cuddled, exchanged family news, swapped cigarettes and quickly returned to their lines. It was to be a number of years before they saw each other again after the war. At one stage during the war, Jack had his appendix taken out by an army Field Surgical Team. After surgery, they gave him dressings, pain killers, antibiotics, cigarettes and left him in a small jungle hut to recover with other soldiers. Then it was back into the fight for Jack. Gary came from tough stock, as he looks back on his life and is amazed how God planned it.

He likes to quote *Psalm 139: Verses 1&2*, "O Lord, you have searched me and you know me. You know when I sit and when I rise: you perceive my thoughts from afar."

Gary is a double survivor for he was saved from oblivion twice. The first escape was when his mother decided not to have her pregnancy with Gary terminated. The second escape came as a complete shock when his mother planned her suicide and murder Gary and his four brothers. The main reason this sad turn of events came about was due to the fact of little money for the family to live on.

Gary's father occasionally gambled at the trots and greyhounds. He raced and bred greyhounds in his younger days. He once had a champion greyhound that was poisoned with bait thrown over the back fence. To make matters more difficult, Gary's father played sport and socialised with his mates at the weekends. He often went to sporting fixtures or watched lawn bowls. This made some weekends extremely lonely for Beryl. There was no respite from the boys. Sometimes, Gary's father would be so drunk. He ended up sick. It was his Gary's mother's task to steady his father and support his forehead while he vomited. Gary's job as the eldest son was to hold the bucket under his father's mouth, to make sure none of the mess went on the floor.

Looking back, Gary says it was probably this experience that acclimatised him to cope with vomit. Later in his life as an ambulance officer, he had to hold a bowl under the chin of many patients who were vomiting. He says this is a task many can't perform without being sick themselves, but he was okay with it.

Gary jokingly asked me, "Nice story before lunch, isn't it?"

Gary's family never owned a car. Neither his dad, nor mum learned to drive or held a driver's licence. Poverty, some gambling and not having a home to call hers, was driving Beryl Raymond to despair. On one occasion Gary's parents were arguing in the kitchen and Gary saw his mother grab a knife from the drawer as she said to her husband.

"One of these days Jack, I'm going to kill all the kids and myself." She yelled, screamed and swore at the time.

Gary's dad said, "Don't be so stupid Oc." 'Oc' was Gary's mother's nickname, short for 'octopus legs' because as a young woman, she had long skinny legs.

The look in her eyes and the tone of her voice put fear deep into Gary and filled his mind. It changed him emotionally. Gary knew she was going to do it. Such fear, that every night Gary lay awake fearing his mother would come in and murder them with a knife. There was a gap beneath the bedroom door and the light shone there. Gary watched wide eyed for his mother's shadow under the door, a murderer's shadow in Gary's eyes. He also listened intently for the creaks in the timber floorboards as another indicator of movement in the house towards his bedroom. Gary was so scared he'd stay awake until he was sure his mother had gone to bed. He thought she might come in and murder them while they slept. Sometimes, when Nanna went to the toilet in the early hours of the morning, Gary would be startled and wake up thinking it was his mother coming to get them. As a result of sometimes not getting proper sleep, he'd fall asleep at his desk at school and get in trouble from teachers. From a very early age, Gary wet the bed on a regular basis. His parent's conflict increased the frequency of bedwetting. He was staying in bed in case he met his mother in the hallway or backyard at night on the way to the outside toilet. He also slept deeply for short periods of time.

At one time Gary's Aunty Phyllis used humour to take the tension the situation.

She laughed and told Gary, "You're going to be a fireman when you grow up because you use your hose to put out fires every night."

Gary loved his Uncle Bill and Aunty Phyllis but was afraid to tell them of his fears as Uncle Bill was a policeman. Gary thought in his child's mind, Uncle Bill would arrest his mum and take her to gaol for threatening to kill him and his brothers.

Frustrated, Gary's mother took him to Doctor Murphy, their local GP. The doctor gave them a machine which had a wire with a 'condom' looking attachment. If Gary started to wet the bed during the night, the machine would react to the dampness, cause a circuit to vibrate, produce a small electric shock in his groin, sound a buzzing alarm and wake him up so that he could get up and go to the toilet, before wetting the bed. This whole process became so full of stress for Gary and he didn't stop the bedwetting. His mother stopped him using it. The doctor said they'd have to wait until he grew out of it. Gary again was too afraid to tell the doctor he was scared of his mother.

One thing added to another. Beryl Raymond was depressed and angry. So depressed, she planned to murder her five boys and suicide. Not by a knife as Gary thought, but in fact, by gas from the stove.

She lied to Doctor Murphy and told him she couldn't sleep. He prescribed sleeping pills. She left the surgery knowing the pills were not for her, but to mix with orange cordial to put her boys to sleep when she gassed them all and herself. At least she didn't want her boys suffering. Besides that, it would prevent the boys from escaping their fate and spoiling their mother's plan.

Gary's mother told him her planning was meticulous and secretive. She rolled up towels with sticky tape to seal the windows and door jams so the gas would stay in the room. She wrote a suicide note and placed it where the police would easily find it, but no one else. She even marked the calendar with a small 'x' on the day when she was going to carry out her desperate plan. It was to be a Sunday when Jack was at cricket and Nanna was going to be out for the day.

Meanwhile, Salvation Army Lieutenant Gwen Fisher, later Gwen Laurence, was door knocking, calling at homes to see if there were any children who would like to go to a new Sunday school. Gary's mum agreed to let them go and they started attending the New Lambton Salvation Army Sunday school, an outpost of the Lambton Salvation Army.

On Saturday 7 October, 1961 there was a Salvation Army Corps (church) anniversary weekend. Gary's mother took her five boys along. Jack didn't go. It was the very night before Gary's mum planned to commit the murder/suicide. Gary says his Mum later explained that while she sat there in the audience that night she planned what she'd do next day. She just wanted to see her boys happy for the last time before they all died. She later knew that God caused her to be there that crucial night. God's perfect planning.

The Corp Officer (minister) was the Late Major Dudley Schoupp, later Colonel, and the guest speaker was Brigadier Gordon Spillet.

Years later, Colonel Schoupp told Gary that after the musical performances, Brigadier Spillet said from the platform, "I know this is a night for the corps anniversary but my heart is heavy because God, through his Holy Spirit, has told me there's someone in this hall tonight that needs two things. Firstly, Christ to forgive them for their sin and secondly, Christ to heal their deep hurts."

Gary's mother thought that was nice but it didn't touch her heart too much at all.

Brigadier continued assertively but gently, "God has just said in my heart this decision must be made tonight as it will not wait until tomorrow. Tomorrow will be too late for you and some others. In Jesus' Name come forward now and receive all that God has for you."

Gary's mother later told him that those words about "tomorrow will be too late for you and some others" by the Brigadier just suddenly pierced her heart with enormous guilt and conviction. She knew God Himself was speaking to her in love and forgiveness through the Brigadier. She hadn't told anybody whatsoever about her murderous plot but it seemed God knew. She said she then realised God was telling her not to complete her suicide/murder and to come to Him for forgiveness.

Brigadier said, "Let's close our eyes and bow in prayer."

The piano was being played. Colonel Schoupp told Gary at this point his mother stood up, looked around, folded her light coat over the seat and cried bitterly. She quickly went forward and fell on her knees at the front of the hall at what's called the 'mercy seat' or 'altar'. Gary remembers her cries and saw her tears drop on the timber seat and floor. A number of ladies from both the Salvation Army and other churches came forward to comfort Gary's Mum and pray with her. Some ladies stroked his mum's hair and others gently patted her back. Gary was confused watching her cry. He and his brothers were worried seeing their mother so upset. Three Salvation Army soldiers, Jack Davis, Len and Ted Randall, went up to Gary and his brothers telling them everything would be alright. Their mother was crying to Jesus. Gary has never forgotten those Salvation Army soldiers and their wives for the good influence they had on him both then and later in his life.

When they finished praying Brigadier said to Gary's mum, "Do you want to tell us what God has done for you tonight? You don't have to, I won't embarrass you."

She said quietly, "I want to. Jesus saved my life and the life of my boys here tonight. Tomorrow, I was going to gas myself and all these boys to death."

There was an audible murmur throughout the hall as shocked people came to grips with what she'd said.

She continued, "Not anymore. God's forgiven me for everything that I've ever done wrong. God's going to help me and my whole family from now on. Jesus has saved me."

The people erupted into applause and celebration. This also happens in heaven too when a sinner comes to Jesus. There was singing and dancing around the hall. A 'Halleluiah Windup,' as the Salvos name it. Then of course, the famous salvo cup of tea and dessert for supper. Gary points out, that from that night his mother dramatically became a changed woman. The yelling and screaming stopped. Even the neighbours noticed the change. No more swearing coming from the Raymond's.

Next morning she said to her husband, "Jack, I want to tell you what I was going to do today." She showed him the towels, pills, calendar and a suicide note explaining what each was for.

He was greatly disturbed and said, "Has it got to this Beryl?"

"Yes Jack it did, but last night at the Salvation Army, I gave my heart and life to Christ. I am going to start going to church. This family is going to be brand new, turn over a new leaf Jack."

Gary's father was deeply moved and he apologised. It really shocked him. He stopped most of his drinking and gambling. The family did more things together. The cricket and the footy didn't take such a big place in his life and, if it did, he took the boys with him. At the football, Gary and his brothers would collect empty drink bottles and cash them in for pocket money. Time to go home, Gary's dad would whistle. Even in a crowd of hundreds of people, the boys knew their dad's whistle and responded immediately.

Gary's mum went into Salvation Army uniform. She learnt to play the piano, guitar, timbrel and became a singer. She also became the Young People's Sergeant Major (head of the Sunday school), led the women's Home League, and was Missionary Sergeant. She was a strong witness for Christ with her love for Him quite evident. She made lemon butter with a secret recipe to raise money for missionaries. She raised lots of money for the Flying Doctor Service as well. She knitted over one hundred stuffed clowns for children's birthdays at the church.

Gary's dad changed too. He was a different man from then on. He was strong, had a great sense of humour and was always 'people friendly.' All the boys became his mates. Gary's father was a little reluctant with Beryl's activity within the Salvation Army as it did take time away from him. He harboured some resentment and only attended church on special occasions only. Gary's mum would try to approach him about Jesus but he would quickly 'shut her down'. She loved him and wanted the best for him. He was a very good man.

Some years later he approached Gary with half a smirk and said, "Well, what do you want the good news or the bad news pal?"

Gary said, "Both."

He said, "The bad news is, I've been diagnosed as having terminal lung cancer. The good news is I've given up smoking!" They both heartily laughed but that was the beginning of a great challenge for Gary watching his father wasting away and dying. Gary prayed with his bedridden dad on many occasions.

One day his dad was visited by Colonel Dudley Schoupp, his former Salvation Army Corps Officer (minister) who challenged him, "Jack you've been a good man. You've lived a good life. Is that right?"

Jack said, "Yes."

Colonel said, "However, you've lived it without Christ. Is that right?"

Jack said, "Yes."

Colonel said, "But Jack, are you going to die without Christ?"

Jack said, "No."

The colonel then led Jack Raymond to Christ and Jack asked that his sin be forgiven through what Jesus did on the cross for him, a free pardon. There and then Gary's father knelt down in his lounge room and accepted Christ as his Saviour after repeating a prayer, after the colonel. Not long after, while dying in hospital, Jack would send Gary around the ward to pray with sick and dying people.

He would say, "Don't worry about me Gary, go and talk to that bloke over there. He needs prayer."

It wasn't long after that Jack died. Gary's mother died some years later, also with cancer.

When she was near the end, Gary said to his mother as a general enquiry, "Are you okay Mum?"

She said, "Yes."

Gary with a subtle challenge said, "Are you sure Mum?"

She looked straight at Gary and said, "Yes Gary, your mother is alright but her overcoat is falling to bits."

The term 'overcoat' refers to her physical body. She told Gary she didn't want to suffer or die in front of anyone as it would distress them.

Gary said, "God, in His mercy, answered her prayer. Mum suddenly died beside her bed near her Bible and was found the next morning by a sister in law. She had lived alone at this stage in her life and the family checked on her daily."

So Gary survived two attempts on his own life. Both attempts controlled by his mother, but prevented by his 'Heavenly Father'.

Gary was truly rescued in the fullest sense. Heaven alone will reveal how many other times Gary came close to death, in the course of his thirty four years in the New South Wales Police Force. Who knows? God knows.

"The Policeman"

As the famous Doctor Luke said of Jesus, "The world could not contain all the stories of Jesus." In the case of retired Chief Inspector Gary Raymond, I discovered there's no end to the stories he can relate from his thirty four years in the New South Wales Police Force. My big challenge was where to draw the line and which stories to select from the wide ranging incidents covered by this one policeman's life. The other challenge was where to start. I could take the approach of Julie Andrews and 'start at the beginning' but no, that would be too commonplace for a very uncommon retired policeman. Uncommon in more ways than one for he's a Christian, a uniformed member of the Salvation Army where he used to play the cornet, tenor horn and flugelhorn, all brass instruments in the band. He's too busy these days to 'practise' or get to 'rehearsals' so the brass gathers dust. Just dive in I said to myself and so that's the way it turned out. I thought that being the author I'd select stories that originally caught my attention. Stunning stories like the day Gary was a high flyer rescuing a person at the top of a television tower in Sydney certainly caught my attention. Gary has been a very public person as the following stories will reveal. Any private life during his police service was, shall it be said, somewhat distracted.

The recent deaths of Gary's wonderful sisters in law Judy, Kevin's wife and Tracey, Brian's wife, due to medical problems have rocked Gary and the family however, they are coping day by day with support from family and friends. Gary said emotionally "We miss them both and think of them each day."

CHAPTER TWO

AND DEEDS MOST DEADLY

 ⌒◯)

"Murderers are not monsters. They're men. And that's the most
frightening thing about them." *Alice Sebold (Writer)*

"The Suitcase Bomb"
Long before the Bali or Boston bombers carried out their horrendous
acts of violence, New South Wales had its own tragic experience
with a murderous act. A '000' call came through while Gary was
working at Wetherill Park Police Station. There was a problem at
Fairfield Heights Shopping Centre. A man with a knife had attacked
someone in a real estate office. A real estate agent was to be found
dead. Police and ambulance officers rushed to the scene. Arriving at
the scene, Gary and his mates saw a man with a knife threatening
police at the scene. A young policeman, Constable 1st Class Brook
Russell, bravely approached the offender with a shield. The shielded
policeman was attacked by the offender who reached around behind
the shield and knifed Brook in the shoulder area. The wounded
Brook and his colleagues overwhelmed and disarmed the offender
without further injury. Brook recovered in hospital.

On investigation it was discovered the man of Chinese origin
lived in a shed which had been converted to a granny flat at Fairfield.
This man was a student in China and had become involved in the
Tiananmen Square revolt. He came to Australia to seek asylum
after fearing reprisal from the communist government. The man
wanted his door lock changed, but the estate agent said it wasn't his

responsibility to replace the lock, it was the tenant. It was then the Chinese man went berserk with anger. He attacked and stabbed the estate agent to death.

Once the offender was subdued and taken into custody it was decided to investigate where he lived under a Search Warrant from the Court. The shed was sparse. It had a bed, a wardrobe and plenty of newspaper and other documentary clips on Chinese oppression, especially the Tiananmen Square student protest killings. These clips were scattered throughout the shed and adorned the walls. Gary and his mates tried to work out the motive for the murder and to determine if there was any evidence that the attack on the estate agent may have been pre-meditated. They looked for clues. As they looked, Gary and his mates discovered a large suitcase on top of a wardrobe.

The suitcase, which was extremely heavy, was placed on the bed and opened. Gary and the others in shock couldn't believe their eyes. Sitting in the suitcase was an Improvised Explosive Device or what you could call 'a terrorist bomb'. What an unexpected challenge for all present. The bomb was made of concrete and embedded with metal shrapnel. It was made up of screws, nails, bolts, nuts, washers, razor blades and much more. Plastic tubing full of explosive powder was also embedded in the concrete circling the device. Gary saw a power source and timing device. He'd looked for trip wires or booby traps but thankfully found none, although it would have been too late anyway had there been one.

Within seconds of his observations, Gary along with other police yelled, over and over again, "Evacuate, evacuate, evacuate."

All the police scrambled out of the shed. There was a hurried exit and all police found adequate cover well away from the shed. They evacuated the neighbourhood. Police and military bomb specialists were called along with the fire brigade and ambulances were also on standby at a safe distance.

Gary realised if the bomb had exploded while they were in the shed, they would have all been killed with little left for their coffins. They would have been literally 'blown to bits' being so close. Talk about a 'near miss'.

Gary then had flashbacks to the time when he had to attend the Hilton Hotel bombing in George Street Sydney about 12.40am 13th February, 1978. Gary's brother, Neil, also attended as a Police Crime Scene Officer. The Commonwealth Heads of Government Regional Meeting was being held at the Hilton. Twelve international leaders were staying at the hotel including Australian Prime Minister Malcolm Fraser. A packaged Improvised Explosive Device had been placed in a garbage container near the front of the hotel. The garbage men unknowingly placed the device in the rear of their truck when they emptied the garbage bin. The bomb exploded violently destroying the rear of the truck. The blast catapulted the truck's rear compactor blade forty or more metres north down George Street. It was a huge explosion. This was a time when, as a member of the Police Rescue Squad, Gary helped the Police Medical Officer to grid, retrieve and package the human remains into plastic bags of those who lost their lives in the explosion. There were bits of bone stripped of flesh and flesh itself everywhere on the road, footpath, through shop windows and on top of shop awnings. In all of his ambulance and police work experience, Gary had never before seen such destruction to human bodies. On that occasion three were killed and eleven injured. Garbage collectors Alex Carter, William Favell and police officer Paul Birmistriw sadly lost their lives. Senior Constable Terry Griffiths was seriously injured and still suffers from those injuries today. Gary remains good mates with Terry as members of the Retired Police Association of NSW.

Gary turned his attention back to the bomb crisis at Fairfield. When the bomb experts arrived they made sure the device was defused. If the bomb had of gone off, in a shopping centre for example, it could have killed hundreds of people with its heavy shrapnel load according to ballistic experts. Another huge surprise followed. A second partially made bomb, the same as the first, was found in another suitcase. The potential deaths may well have been doubled had both devices been detonated together in the same place or separate places.

It turned out the offender had read about the Chinese Premier and other high ranking Chinese officials were planning a visit to Australia. He saw an opportunity to reap revenge and havoc on the Chinese government by using these explosive devices during that visit. The fact that he lost his temper with the estate agent meant his hideous plot was discovered and thankfully stopped in its tracks. Most certainly Gary and his mates were thankful to God for what was a narrow escape. As expressed to me many times, Gary even today continues to thank God for that 'near miss'. The offender was convicted and gaoled for a long time.

"Stomped and Dead"

The police received a call to go to a caravan park at Parklea in western Sydney. A woman had called '000' to say she'd found her boyfriend slumped in the shower.

She said, "I think he's unconscious."

The police found him dead. The Maori woman was arrested shortly after not far from the caravan park. She was walking along the road not far from where the body was found. The woman was in a dazed state and emotional. She was taken into custody and Gary and his mate went to the crime scene. On arrival, they found a man slumped in a shower recess. He was pronounced dead by ambulance officers.

The deceased had apparently gone to the bedroom, taken off his clothes and staggered into the shower. As they looked, they saw marks all over his head and body. Surprisingly, he had shoe sole imprints all over his face and head, signs of being stomped. It took a while before Gary and his mate could interview the woman who'd had a few drinks and was most upset and couldn't stop crying. At this stage nobody had told her the man in the shower, her fiancé, was actually dead.

Gary introduced himself and said, "Has anyone spoken to you about your fiancé and his condition?" "No, is he alright?"

Gary gave her a criminal caution that she was not obliged to say anything.

Then he said, "I'm really sorry to inform you that he's dead."

She immediately had an anxiety attack.

She was beyond herself, hysterical, crying and saying, "I don't believe it. I don't believe it. I didn't mean to kill him just teach him a lesson before I left him".

She was in disbelief, denial and angry with herself. Gary tried to pacify her but she was in no state to be interviewed regarding the death of her fiancé. Gary realised that while she was in such a state it would not have been a fair interview. He told his partner that they would not conduct an interview until she had calmed down and sobered up. An hour or so later she had calmed down. Gary decided that the interview could now go ahead. The sad story by the suspect was revealed. Some months earlier, her younger sister had come over from New Zealand. She was about fourteen years old then. She stayed in the caravan with her sister and the deceased, later returning to New Zealand. Once back in New Zealand, she revealed that while staying with the couple, the deceased man had sexually assaulted her several times by having intercourse with her against her will.

The woman didn't believe her sister and said, "You're lying, he wouldn't do that. He wouldn't be capable of doing anything like that. He is a good man"!

The deceased had strongly denied it at that time. The young girl was called a liar and a troublemaker.

At the time the deceased said, "She's making everything up. She's infatuated with me and she's trying to break us up, so don't take any notice of her."

On the day of the death, the deceased and the suspect went to a party in the caravan park. The two of them had far too much alcohol to drink. On the way home, they started to argue about something, and in the heat of the moment he admitted to sexually assaulting her younger sister. He then laughed loudly and threatened to leave her. The suspect was shocked to the core and controlled herself at that moment, but when they staggered back to their caravan, she completely lost control and unleashed her fury against him. She punched him, pushed him over, screamed at him and kicked him because of what he'd done to her sister. The man ended up on the floor and while he was on the floor, she violently stomped and jumped on him with her shoes on. He was stomped all over, especially his head and face.

She then screamed, "Get out of here. I never want to see you again you rotten bastard of a man. I hate you!"

She backed off and sat down on a chair sobbing. He stood up and decided to get a shower. A few minutes later the woman heard a loud heavy thump in the shower and found him on the floor unresponsive. She ran to a neighbour and called '000'. An ambulance turned up, but the man was dead by the time it arrived.

The post mortem results showed that the man died of a cerebral haemorrhage. The pathologist who conducted the autopsy couldn't tell whether he died as a result of the stomping or his fall in the shower whilst intoxicated. The charge was changed from the original one of murder and downgraded to manslaughter.

After all, as Gary put it, "We knew she had not intended to kill him just punish him for sexually assaulting her younger sister. That's manslaughter at law. No intent to kill."

When the official interview was totally over and formal enquiries had been completed Gary engaged the woman in a personal conversation. The woman was shaking and crying.

Gary asked, "Do you have any Christian background by any chance"?

"Yes. God will never forgive me for what I've done."

Gary said, "I'm going to pray for you as I know God, in Christ on the cross, has already forgiven you."

"Yes please do, I'm scared," she begged.

Gary prayed for her and comforted her. She just wanted to punish herself. She stayed in custody overnight, went to court the next morning and was granted conditional bail. The Salvation Army got involved. Gary and his wife Michelle took a special interest in the young woman and took her to church. She was alone without family. She would sit in church between Gary and Michelle with her whole body shaking. She was an emotional mess.

Even though Gary was the arresting officer he took on another role of Christian comforter. Gary knew how to carefully balance and combine his Christian faith with his police work and not offend anyone. There was no conflict of interest, just a well balanced caring police officer. Gary always acted appropriately in his behaviour by always having other people present when he dealt with people in such circumstances as these, in this case, his wife Michelle. The young woman's family finally came over from New Zealand and gave her good support.

The matter went to court and she was acquitted of both murder and manslaughter because a connection could not be found to his death between the stomping and the intoxicated fall in the shower. In other words, it could not be proven she was responsible for his death. The fact he was heavily intoxicated played a part in his death. The young Maori woman was let off. She thanked God for what He had done for her during this dark crisis in her life. She went to work in a country hospital as a nurse's aide and regularly attends church today. The last Gary heard she was trying to find out what God wanted her to do with her life. Gary said, "That's what being a Christian police officer is about. Some might find it hard to understand you can be a law enforcer and minister to people at the same time. Just because I was a cop, doesn't mean I give up my Christ given compassion for victims, witnesses, offenders and their families as well."

"In the Heat of the Moment"

Hurt. What a word? Who can describe the hurt caused by murder? There are no nice murders. Regardless of where, how or why, murder is murder and there's always hurt and heartbreak for those left behind. Some murders are planned and deliberate. Some are the result of a burst of anger and some involve alcohol or drugs, such as the murder of Michael Martin.

Detective Sergeant Gary Raymond and his mates were dispatched to a house in Virginia Street, Blacktown. A report had come through of a murder. A youth had discovered his neighbour's blood soaked body. When Gary walked in, maintaining a safe distance to avoid crime scene contamination, he saw the body of a man whose throat had been cut. Blood was everywhere on everything. The place was a mess with broken beer and wine bottles strewn around.

"Some murder scenes are neat and clean. This one was very bloody, messy and dirty," Gary said.

Near the body of the male person was a pair of scissors, a bent knife and fork. It was clear there must have been a violent struggle between the killer and victim. Gary quickly realised the stab wounds on the victim were probably made by a sharp instrument or two. There were even stab wounds to the head. Gary also noticed shoeprints in blood were all over the place showing that someone had even walked over the lounge leaving bloodied impressions on the cushions. Footprints in blood were also observed to and from the kitchen. It was clear that the offender had run backwards and forwards from the kitchen to the lounge room picking a range of different weapons from the kitchen drawer to use on the deceased. The viciousness of the murder told Gary the offender was certainly out to kill the victim and not just to do harm or defend themselves.

Michael's gay partner was immediately ruled out of the investigation since he was away working with the railway as a train steward and had a strong alibi. His young neighbour gave a good description including the fact that the offender had a missing front tooth. Another line of enquiry led to a local pub. It appeared that Michael and a man named Jason had been in a pub at Blacktown the previous night. The suspect Jason had a front tooth missing. The young fellow who reported the crime said he saw a man in the deceased's house before the murder who smelt of alcohol and who had a front tooth missing. A search for weapons was carried out and a knife was found down the street in a gutter. It matched the fatal cut in Michael Martin's throat. It didn't take long to identify the suspect, find him at his home and arrest him for the crime. Shoes were found that matched the footprints beside the deceased and on the lounge chair fabric. Michael's blood was later found on the suspect's shoes even though the suspect's mother had washed them in a failed effort to eliminate the blood.

Jason admitted they'd been drinking at a pub. They decided to get a change of clothes from Michael's home and go back out drinking in a more up-market pub. Michael told Jason he could borrow some of his clothes for the night out. Jason's story was that as they were getting changed, Michael made some homosexual advances to him. He became angry and lost his temper. The police knew it was a tall story. To plead 'self defence' or 'provocation' didn't fit the physical evidence photographed or collected. The viciousness of the attack went far beyond the bounds of 'self defence'. Rather it seemed more likely that Michael caught Jason looking around for money or valuables in the house that he could steal. Jason was convicted of murder and received a lengthy gaol sentence. He showed no remorse for his dreadful crime. Heather Martin, Michael's mother and her partner couldn't believe Michael would have made advances of a homosexual nature. Michael was in a happy relationship and lived with his male partner. The murder of her son meant Heather struggled to cope. She found support by joining the Homicide Victims Support Group in Sydney. Garry and Peg Lynch, parents of murdered Anita Cobby, were in the same group. For one person the hurt was eased a little by being able to help others who were hurting. Part of Gary's ministry as a Christian cop, was supporting the family and friends of those left behind after the death of a loved one, no matter who they were or what the circumstances.

"How shall we tell them?"

The attractive nurse stepped off the train at Blacktown. It was a hot summer night in February 1986. She was to phone her father to get him to meet her at the station and drive her home. No public phones were working so she decided to walk. After a happy time at a Lebanese restaurant in Redfern with two female nursing friends, she felt good. All was well. All was right with the world. She'd walk to her parents as the weather was fine. As she left the train, she had no idea what monstrous things were to happen to her within minutes. She would never reach home, however was about to reach the end of her life instead. For the nurse it was a routine walk, one she'd done many times being raised in Blacktown. She could not have known that this night was any different to any other. There was no need to disturb her parents. 'If only' she'd be able to call her father with a phone that worked, but life cannot be lived backwards on 'if only.' Gary wonders if the hoodlums who broke the public phones, ever knew the consequences of their malicious damage.

Meanwhile, five intoxicated men, all with criminal records, were on the prowl looking for a woman to abduct and abuse. Too lazy and too heartless to form proper relationships with women, instead they would drag one off the street to exert their power and control. However, not even the most hardened human beings and police officers could have expected them to act the way they did against this innocent victim. During a steady walk in a safe Sydney suburb during a pleasant Australian summer's evening enter five evil men in a stolen car, a car which slowed beside the walking nurse. When the car stopped, a crime followed. Julia Sheppard, author of *Someone Else's Daughter*, believes it was a crime so shocking it should never be forgotten.

As Anita's parents, the late Garry and Grace Lynch, waited at home for the arrival of their daughter. Detective Gary Raymond, like the nurse and her parents, had no idea of the tragic circumstances that would soon engulf them all.

"It is the suddenness of violent crime that takes you by surprise sometimes. Peace to mayhem in a second," Gary said.

It was not a long walk from the Blacktown Railway Station to the Lynch home which was why it became so hard to believe there could be disaster along the way for this attractive young woman. When five men, high on a cocktail of alcohol and drugs, and fuelled by lust, start looking for trouble, anything can happen. The nurse, Anita Cobby, could never in her wildest dreams have even begun to imagine the evil that was about to launch itself upon her. The foul deeds that would be committed were worse than any horror film Anita may have seen at a cinema or read about in a book. The gang of five was led by John Travers, a person who had been in endless trouble with the police since the age of thirteen. His four followers were like willing slaves that dark night as they drove around the

Blacktown streets seeking whom they might treat as some object of their lustful desires. For Travers, a predator, rape was his favourite crime. He saw Anita as she walked along Newton Road.

Suddenly she became his target. "Stop the car."

The men needed no second command. They pounced on Anita. She shrieked with fear, struggled and kicked as she was lifted and shoved without ceremony into the rear of the car. It sped off with its unwilling and terrified captive. A gruesome degrading process began. From the moment she was dragged into the car, indecent acts followed. She was told to strip. She refused. Her clothes were ripped off as she was held down. Money was taken from her purse. They obtained petrol without paying and drove off whilst Anita was kept quiet on the floor in the back of the stolen car. Since there was no phone call to pick her up at the station, Anita's parents thought their daughter had decided to stay in the city with friends.

Next day, after a nursing sister from Sydney Hospital called to find out why Anita hadn't reported for work, her father went to Blacktown Police Station. He reported his daughter missing. Out went a description. Anita was a thin build, 175cm tall, black wavy hair, hazel eyes and a light olive complexion. Blacktown police had already received reports of a girl being abducted in a car that night in the area of Newton Road. They were beginning to put two and two together. One of the most extensive Australian manhunts was on. Time was of the essence. Could she be found before it was too late?

When Detective Gary Raymond heard about what happened to Anita Cobby, like many others, he found it hard to believe. Even after five years in the ambulance service and over ten years in police rescue he thought he'd seen it all. Was it possible that in Sydney in the 1980's, a woman could be restrained, bashed, raped, tortured, brutalised, have her throat slashed so badly she was almost decapitated, have her fingers broken – and have all this happen while she was still alive? Defence wounds on her hands and fingers proved that she had courageously fought with her attackers even when her throat was being cut by Travers.

Then to discover her body was just dumped in mud and grass in a lonely dairy cattle paddock for a farmer to find. Actually, a herd of dairy cows first found her body. They gathered around her almost like a protective cordon. When the dairy farmer went to investigate the strange animal behaviour, he found her. Who could do this to another human being displaying no mercy, respect or feelings, and why?

Gary's thoughts turned to the police who had to tell Anita's ex-husband and parents that a body had been found and was believed to be Anita's. She was no longer a missing person, but sadly found and destroyed by murder. The missing person investigation had regrettably turned into a homicide investigation, a worst nightmare for the family and police.

The police probably thought, "How can we tell them that all that's left of their beautiful daughter is these broken and bloody remains?"

Gary flashed back to the many times, when as a police officer, he'd had to knock on a door to tell a family their loved one or loved ones were not coming home. He used to pray, swallow hard, take deep breaths and blow out hard as he approached the front door. Then he had to watch a stunned family or friends go into shock as he delivered the terrible news. The news was so final. No replays to change things or ease the pain of grief. It was often late at night or the early hours of the morning when people were awakened from their sleep and expected to comprehend what Gary was telling them. Often children, babies or dogs in the house woken by police door knocking added to the already hard job. Then he watched and listened as the terrible news was delivered. Gary will never forget the gasps, screams or guttural moans as people received the news. Tenderly, with God's help he comforted the people and often prayed with them. He'd then wait for more reactions such as denial, disbelief, anger, bargaining and sometimes physically fainting. Some would throw things, kick things, hit walls or tear things. It was like the family was hit by a freight train they didn't know was coming.

Although sometimes with drunks, drug users, crazy drivers or gang members, the family would actually say, "We knew one day or night this knock on the door would come. We're not surprised."

Gary said it was the worst part of policing, yet in another way the best part in his Christian outreach bringing people into the presence of a loving and understanding God during the worst time in their lives. Gary often went back to the house when he finished duty to give further comfort, advice and prayer.

That wasn't the case with the Lynch or Cobby family. The knock on the door had no forewarning, although Anita's father had inkling that something was wrong with Anita's disappearance. The shock still resounds whenever Anita's name is mentioned. The sheer horror of what was to be revealed to Anita's parents is hard for us to even start to imagine.

At the time of the murder, Gary was out of Sydney on an investigation with Detective Tony 'Muddy' Waters. They were recalled urgently back to Blacktown Police Station. Once there, Gary saw photos, gathered information and investigated suspects. His task was to find out as much as possible about individuals who'd recently been released from gaol, mental health units or juvenile institutions that may have the Modus Operandi and be capable of committing such a crime.

Gary also sorted through local criminals who had violent backgrounds. Informants were spoken to by Gary in case they had some 'inside' information on the murder. Even seasoned criminals in the area promised Gary they would 'give up' the gang to the police if they found out where they were. Not only the police network, but the criminal network went into overdrive. Meanwhile, Tony Waters joined the senior detectives in the hunt for the killers. A sense of urgency hovered over the detectives, because while the criminals were on the loose, they could rape or kill again— especially if they thought they'd get caught and spend big time in gaol. They may use their short freedom to cram in as much 'pleasure' as possible. Gary and the other detectives were afraid the offenders might go on a 'frenzy feed' of violence before they were captured, a last perverted pleasure seeking fling before going to gaol.

Everyone close to the crime saw them as monstrous criminals who attacked a woman in an uncontrolled frenzied outburst. They'd acted like a pack of wild animals, although wild animals have a reason to attack for food, territory or self defence. This pack didn't have that reason or any other reason except their self gratification and evil lust. They must be caught, and caught soon. It showed Gary how mankind's sin could be the cause of such ungodly demonic behaviour in union with man's depraved Adamic nature. Even in the criminal's demented so called 'code of conduct', you never hurt a child, nurse, nun, Salvation Army lady or elderly person. This mob didn't even adhere to that. The biggest impact of the Cobby crime was that the offenders were still on the loose.

Looking back Gary said, "There was palpable fear throughout the Sydney western area. You could just about smell the fear in the air. People were hypervigilant on the street, especially at night. The crime might be repeated over and over again before the offenders were taken into custody. The crime was taken so seriously, many locked their doors, windows and stayed home. Some even obtained weapons, whether legally or not. Men were protective of their wives and daughters. They met them at taxi ranks, railway or bus stations and took them straight home. Some workplaces employed security guards to escort women from work to car parks or return. Every woman in the area was terrified they might not be alive next morning. It was a real threat, not just perceived."

Gary has never seen people so scared and angry. Even the toughest blokes around the streets of Blacktown were anxious. This also affected police who left their families at home as they investigated the crime. Many police sent their family to relatives or friends' houses until the offenders were arrested. Gary kept a check on his wife Michelle who was home alone. He stressed on her forcefully and frequently the security measures she had to take. All this added to the stress of the manhunt.

Along with other police officers, Gary attended a briefing in the detective's office. Doors were closed to prevent other police seeing what was coming. Photographs of the crime scene and autopsy were shown to the investigators.

He said, "As I looked at the photographs, I couldn't believe human beings could treat another human being in such a way. The paddock had become a torture chamber under the stars. Even though we looked at the photos forensically, we couldn't help but contemplate what Anita went through."

As he gazed at the photos, a shiver rippled through his spine. The hairs on his neck were just about standing on edge.

"How could they have done this?" he kept repeating to himself.

It was outside all the detectives' mindsets. Gary, a hardened ambulance and police veteran, was used to seeing human remains after fatal incidents or illnesses killed them but on this occasion, he was moved to tears. With Anita's murder, the sheer force of the attack on this innocent nurse beggared description. Gary, when sick or injured in the past, had experienced nurses treating him, other police and community members in hospital with compassion and dedication. Anita didn't deserve this. Words failed him. If some ravenous beast had been responsible it might have been easier to cope, but humans? The sheer impact of the attack on Anita was hard to believe.

John Travers had a distinct teardrop tattoo under his left eye. Maybe in the moonlight Anita saw this teardrop. By this she may have been able to identify her attackers had she survived. Travers thought it far too risky. This fuelled his lust for blood to eliminate the witness. The others didn't bother to stop him. Even a wild animal could hardly have ripped Anita apart in the way he did. As for the crime scene, the remains of Nurse Anita were flung down into the long grass like a rag doll. Those remains so mutilated while the fiends, having done their worst, slunk away numb without a conscience.

As the investigation proceeded, a neighbour saw clothes being burnt in a backyard the morning after the crime had been committed. There was also a report of a stolen car. Travers was arrested. As information came in, the search was on for where the other offenders might stay. Who might shelter them? There were many tips by phone, others by people going to the police station. The Tactical Response Group was called in. After a tip, police sped off in convoy to a place where the suspects might be. As Gary looked at the crime scene photos, he found it hard to believe anything like the rape and murder of Anita Cobby could happen. It was a somewhat isolated place with dairy farming and grazing land with eucalypt trees. It also had long grass which helped to hide the crime scene. It was not that far from the Great Western Highway, a road with thousands of vehicles passing daily. Yet far enough away so that no one heard a cry for help as Anita fought for her life.

There is never an excuse for rape. Nobody has the right to rape another. It has been said that "rape is the only crime in which the victim becomes the accused" (Freda Adler). Sadly someone once said that 'rape is the easiest charge to make, and the most difficult to prove'.

From a Christian viewpoint we must be reminded of the words of Eli Khamarov, "To admit there's no God is to provide free license to pillage and rape with clear conscience." One thing is certain, there is no way a Christian can rape, for it takes away another person's right to live without fear.

A ring was taken from Anita's finger. Detective Sgt Ian Kennedy had the responsibility of taking that tiny ring to the Lynch home. The ring was identified as belonging to Anita. Garry Lynch was taken to Westmead hospital. He identified the broken and bruised body of his daughter. As it was a Coroner's homicide investigation, no contamination of the body was allowed which meant a father was unable to embrace his daughter's body at the City Mortuary. The ache was unfathomable and hurt Garry Lynch deeply, but he understood.

A hidden microphone, obtained on a Supreme Court Warrant, was carried by an informant to the cell complex at Blacktown Police and she recorded Travers confession of his deadly deeds after he was arrested.

At one stage, when Gary was back at the police station, he helped the other officers by buying takeaway food and made coffee for them after they had conducted a raid. The offenders had eluded police before they arrived on that raid. Gary heard a banging noise coming from the locker room. It was a loud metallic echoing sound like thunder. He went to the door of the locker room and stood for a moment amazed. There was a detective pounding his fists into a metal locker door. Gary paused and just watched. He didn't know what the punching was all about.

The detective turned, looked at Gary and with gritted teeth and an angry look said, "We missed the bastards."

He was so angry and scared that the offenders had got away.

Gary said, "Don't worry mate, you'll get them. Come and have a coffee."

Gary looked at the detective's hands. They were red after pounding the locker. This detective was angry, not only that the killers had got away, but angry that they might commit further crimes. We didn't want more victims. It was frustrating and beyond belief that later they found out the people who harboured the offenders were women.

Gary felt sorry for the detective, but even sorrier for Anita's parents who were at the police station. Garry and Grace Lynch just had blank looks on their faces.

Gary Raymond asked them, "Can I get you something to eat or drink?"

Anita's father said, "No thanks Gary. I want information. Information, no matter how bad it is that you and your colleagues find out and I want to know every bit of information. Some people don't want to know or need to know. I want to know and I need to know everything."

When all the offenders were subsequently caught, Gary was away from the police station following a lead. As he arrived back at the station the offenders were being interviewed upstairs. They were charged with murder and other offences.

When the charging process was finished an announcement came over the police station public address system, "All available police to urgently assemble at the front of the police station for crowd control."

Gary hurriedly put on his gun and handcuffs under his suit coat. The entire Kildare Road was packed with a crowd of about three hundred or so people yelling obscenities and threats towards the perpetrators. Gary has never seen anything like it before or since. What amazed him was the composition of the crowd. All ages, many nationalities and both genders. The terror and rage on their faces was noticeable yet with some relief, the offenders had been captured and charged. It was a crowd yelling threats of reprisal and wanting 'an eye for an eye.' Westpoint Shopping Centre is opposite the police station and word had spread through the media and by word of mouth that the Cobby killers were at Blacktown Police Station. Hanging from the roof of the shopping centre were ropes with nooses at the end. The area was in lock down. The police virtually faced a modern day 'lynch mob.' As the police vans came out with the offenders going to gaol after court, Gary recalls the crowd surged forward yelling threats.

Along with other police he yelled, "Move back, Move back."

Physical encounters started occurring between the crowd and the police. People looked 'straight through' Gary and continued to push forward. They were puffing with anger and grinding their teeth. They wanted a look at the offenders and give them a 'mouth full' of abuse.

An elderly lady of about eighty years old looked at Gary and said as she pointed to the nooses hanging from the building opposite, "That's what we're going to do with them and you're going to let us do it."

The rhythmic cries of, "Hang the bastards" became very loud.

One man looked at Gary and yelled, "Do you have a daughter? I do, let me get at the mongrels and string 'em up."

There can be no excuse for the savage attack on Anita and savage it was. Savage in intent and savage in the way the crimes were executed. For John Travers, the word mercy was unknown, even in the last act of throat slitting. Even though it was a wild cowardly act, we couldn't allow street justice to prevail and the 'lynch mob' was restrained and controlled with a lot of difficulty and high emotion. Finally the police cars moved away and the crowd slowly dispersed but Gary has never forgotten the scene. He is convinced, beyond a shadow of doubt, that had the police lost control of the crowd, they would have busted the offenders from the vans and hung them all. One of the most amazing things about the whole Cobby killing is the sheer grace shown by Anita's late parents and the fact her father served on the Serious Offenders Review Board for some years after the murder. One thing he did stipulate was that if any of his daughter's killers came before the Board, he would not attend as he had a 'conflict of interest'.

For Garry Lynch, the loss of his daughter pained him to his dying day.

He said, "It feels like a dagger goes through your heart."

Grace Lynch said, "It was an experience beyond thinking."

For a Christian like Gary Raymond, to put the Anita Cobby murder into perspective has been hard. As he turned to the scriptures he thought perhaps there's help in the words of *Romans 8:22 (NIV)* where it says, *"We know that the whole creation has been groaning as in the pains of childbirth right up to the present time."*

Gary said, "After all, there's no way in which God can be blamed for the crimes of the Travers gang. This gang of five made their decision against God's will and the consequences of their sins were catastrophic."

Then again a further look at the Bible helps to explain how people have strayed away from God's way. *(Romans 3: 10-18 NIV) "There is none righteous, not even one; there is no one who understands, no one who seeks God. All have turned away; they have together become worthless; there is no one who does good, not even one. Their throats are open graves; their tongues practice deceit. The poison of vipers is on their lips. Their mouths are full of cursing and bitterness. Their feet are swift to shed blood; ruin and misery mark their ways. And the way of peace they do not know. There is no fear of God before their eyes."* Does this offer some explanation? Surely it well describes those who have no time for God and God was the last person in the mind of those five when they attacked Anita Cobby?

The way the gang sniggered together in court later meant they probably laughed as they left Anita lying broken and smashed to pieces in the muddy grass field.

Judge of the Supreme Court, Justice Alan Maxwell was later to describe the crime, "One of the most horrifying physical and sexual assaults. This was a calculated killing done in cold blood."

At the trial, the judge said, "Wild animals are given to assault and killing for the purpose of survival. Not so these prisoners. They assaulted in a pack for satisfying their lust, and killed for the purpose of preventing identification".

As television presenter Steve Liebmann put it, the Cobby case is, "A scar that will never go away. Justly the files on the accused were marked, never to be released."

For Gary there's hope. As a Christian he believes things will not always stay as they are. A change is on the way, *"God will wipe every tear from their eyes. There will be no more death or mourning or crying or pain, for the old order of things has passed away." (Revelation 21: 3-4 NIV).* The memory of Anita Cobby should and must be kept alive. Anita's parents were never the same after her murder. The dark deeds of that night should never be shrouded in mystery, but kept clearly in the light of truth. A woman was violated in a most despicable way. We should never, ever, let this act be forgotten. Women were not created as playthings but as helpmates. One aspect to emerge is that Michael Murdock has become a committed Christian whilst in gaol and attends chapel regularly. One only prays that the other four involved with the Cobby case, do the same as Michael.

"Tess Murdered at Five"

One of the saddest experiences during his 34 year police career was whenever Gary Raymond had to speak with parents after a child had been injured or killed especially murdered. Such was the case when 5 year old Tess Debrincat was shot in May 1987. Gary was called to her home in Quakers Hill a Sydney suburb. Tess was dead on her kitchen floor. She'd been shot as she stood in the kitchen making a sandwich. The shooter had walked from a stolen car, sneaked up and fired a shotgun through the closed front door. He ran back to the car and escaped. The pellets went through the door and hit Tess in the eye and head. She dropped to the floor and died immediately in front of her parents. What a horrific sight for any parents. Gary tried to comfort the distraught parents. He later discovered the shooting had been arranged by a man in exchange for heroin to frighten the Debrincat family after a neighbourhood dispute about industrial refrigeration noise in a residential area. The house across the road was also peppered with gunfire, apparently over the same matter, thankfully with no one injured.

As a result of some excellent detective work, Gary and his team arrested the shooter Glen Thomas Bessant who was gaoled in June 1989 for Tess's death. The sawn-off shotgun was found by Gary and others buried in a backyard wrapped in a breakfast cereal packet. The driver of the stolen getaway car and an accomplice were also gaoled. The man who arranged 'the hit' has, up to this time, eluded justice. The offenders refused to give evidence against him in court. The old 'code of silence' rears its ugly head again. Gary prays that Glen Bessant will one day give evidence in court against the crime's organiser.

Gary said, "Justice sometimes moves slowly, but it moves and never stops".

Gary will never forget seeing the little girl's pellet ridden eye and head as her body lay on the mortuary slab.

He said with tears in his eyes, "Senseless loss of a life. What for, a neighbourhood dispute? There is something awful when you see a child involved in a crime or other tragedy. It was an unnecessary waste of a little life. Who knows what Tess would have done with her life? God knows."

Gary passionately added, "You don't have to tell a cop the world's a mess. The book of Genesis in the Bible clearly tells us sin came into the world when Adam and Eve blatantly disobeyed God. Death, sin, bloodshed and suffering were the result. Before that, creation was perfect and so was our relationship with God. We are all cursed and guilty of our sin until we come to Christ for forgiveness putting our faith and trust in Him to save us. What Jesus did by dying on the cross and His resurrection from the dead, proves He is God the Son. Jesus also promised He is returning soon to make things right. Get ready."

"Christmas Dinner with Tears"

The first Christmas Day that Gary was free from Police duties for seven years meant his wife Michelle was more than excited. Because Michelle and Gary had no children, he worked on many Christmas Days to allow his mates with children to have the day off to open their gifts at home Christmas morning. Michelle and Gary planned to have a pleasant Christmas dinner at home with family members. This was not a working day and he wasn't even on call. Gary and Michelle were excitingly preparing the house for their guests. Gary arranged the extra chairs and put two tables together while Michelle was busy cooking, preparing salads and getting all the trimmings ready. The phone rang. Michelle pleasantly answered.

It was a call from the Blacktown Police station. "Can I talk to Gary?"

"He's off duty and not even on call."

"Well we need to talk to him about something urgently."

When Gary picked up the phone he learned that the body of a young female had been found wrapped up in carpet. The body had been dumped in a bush reserve.

Gary replied, "I'm not working and I'm not even on call. You'll have to get someone else."

"But Gary, the boss said it's a murder and experienced detectives like you are needed."

Gary argued for a while as Michelle watched and listened with an anguished look on her face.

She was mouthing the words towards Gary, "Tell them you're off duty and you are expecting your family for Christmas dinner."

Gary tried again to 'worm' his way out of the call out.

Finally, Gary had to obey his call to duty and do what he was told. As could be expected, Michelle was extremely disappointed and upset that her husband had to go to work, particularly that day. Gary changed into his suit, kissed Michelle and wished her a 'Blessed Christmas' and went down to the police station where they'd arrested the dead woman's husband.

Gary found out that the husband and wife had argued about Christmas Day arrangements that morning. In a fit of temper, she grabbed a saucepan of boiling water from the stove and flung it over her husband. Shocked, scalded and in pain, he had a sudden rage and grabbed his wife around her throat, lifted her feet off the floor and before he knew it, had strangled her to death. In fear and panic he wrapped her body in carpet, tied it up, drove to nearby bush and dumped it. He certainly didn't expect the body to be found so quickly. After dumping the body he went to his family's house for Christmas. He was extremely distraught. When they asked where his wife was, he couldn't or wouldn't explain. The family knew something was gravely wrong and after some discussions, the offender confessed and the police were called. The offender took police to the body and a forensic crime scene was set up. His panel van was also seized as the body was transported in the rear of it.

After such a crime, Gary was surprised the offender had no criminal history, not even a notable traffic offence against his name. In police terms a 'clean skin'? He'd been a hard working man. He'd gone to the Philippines where he married his wife. When Gary and his detective mate interviewed the man, he was extremely upset over the fact he'd killed his wife. He told Gary in tears he'd not intended to kill her. During the interview he told Gary he reacted badly and lost control when his wife threw the boiling water over him. When he discovered she was dead, he acted in fear and dumped her body. The crime scene, booking the body into the morgue, interview and paperwork took most of the day and night for Gary.

Meanwhile, Michelle had rung the police station and asked if Gary had eaten any dinner. The answer was a resounding no. She realised God must have had a purpose in taking her Gary away from the Christmas family dinner. She said she loved Gary and they would make it up one way or another.

Michelle was an amazing support for Gary in his police work and now his retirement work. She is a real friend and confidant when Gary needs to vent his feelings. Because of her love for God and Gary, she made a lot of sacrifices allowing him to do his work. Gary was often away from home for long periods of time, day and night doing rescue work and then investigating crimes.

Gary told me, "In some marriages, they spend all day together and remain superficial, but Michelle and I have a deep marriage and our time together is very meaningful and close."

Later that afternoon, Gary had just finished the interview with the offender and was preparing the murder brief for court when there was an unexpected gentle knock on the detective's office staff back door. When Gary opened the door he saw Michelle standing there with three plates covered with silver foil.

She said, "Here are three Christmas dinners. There's one for you, one for your police partner and one for the man you've arrested." Gary thanked, kissed and wished her a Happy Christmas. He again apologised for being called out. She gently and carefully assured him it was okay.

Gary took the meals into the interview room, gave one to his partner and said to the offender, "Here's your Christmas dinner mate. Try to eat it as you're going into custody soon."

It was a large Christmas dinner, one with all the luscious trimmings. The offender simply stared at the meal. Gary and his partner ate quickly for they were both very hungry. It had been a long day. The offender however didn't eat.

He looked at Gary and asked with a quiet trembling voice, "Where did this come from. It doesn't look like gaol food to me?"

"My wife brought it in for us from home".

"Does she know I killed my wife this morning?"

"Yes, I told her."

"Why did she bring a murderer a Christmas dinner?"

"Because we're both Christians in the Salvation Army and we do care for you."

"I don't deserve this."

"Look mate, Jesus died on the cross to forgive your sins and mine to take our punishment and pay the price. We didn't deserve that, but in His love and grace, He did it anyway. That was His grace in action towards us. As a matter of fact mate, I've been silently praying for you since you were arrested. God has forgiven you not only for what you did this morning, but for all the sins you've ever committed and are going to commit."

The offender slightly raised his voice, swore at Gary and said. "After what I did this morning God wants to forgive me? I don't think so Mr Raymond, I'll burn in hell. That's what He'll do to me."

Gary gently replied, "When He died on the cross mate, He had you in mind as well as me and He has forgiven you and deeply desires to save you from an eternity in hell." "As I said Mr Raymond, I don't think so."

"Well that's what the Bible says, not me."

All went quiet. There was no further talk. The man started to slowly pick away at his Christmas dinner. Then something on the man's plate caught the corner of Gary's eye. Gary saw the dark brown gravy move. Something dented the gravy. It was sort of pulsing. It was kind of weird. As Gary looked intently, it suddenly dawned on him that this small movement was caused as the offender's tears dropped into the Christmas dinner gravy.

Gary broke the silence, "What are you thinking mate?"

The man looked up with red eyes, loaded with tears running down his cheeks, "Are you trying to tell me Mr Raymond, that I killed my wife this morning and Jesus wants to forgive me this afternoon?"

"Yes. He already has on the cross at Calvary".

"It's too good to be true for me."

"His love, grace and mercy are certainly too good to be true mate, but are true."

With that the man started to cry more heavily and loudly. It was like a deep bellowing noise. He then gently moved off his chair and knelt beside it right there in the detective's interview room and begged Jesus to forgive him, not only for killing his wife, but for all the things he'd done wrong during his life. Gary then prayed with him and confirmed that the man had received Jesus as his Saviour and started his 'faith journey' with God.

After the charging process, Gary again prayed with the offender as he placed him in the cell for the night. The offender said he felt devastated with what had happened however, knew he was forgiven. The 'cop' and 'crook' both adored a marvellous forgiving Saviour.

When Gary finally arrived home late that night, everyone had left.

He told Michelle all about the offender and she said, "I knew God had a purpose for calling you in to work today. I didn't like it one bit, but I knew there was plan. God was up to something."

A prolonged hug confirmed their thoughts and feelings. They then had Christmas leftovers and shared the rest of their Christmas Day experiences.

When the case went to court, the accused was convicted of manslaughter not murder, for he didn't 'intend' to kill his wife. He received a reasonably short sentence given the circumstances of 'provocation'.

Shortly after the death, the dead woman's family arrived from the Philippines. They went to Blacktown Police Station and met Gary. As they talked over coffee, they told him their daughter had been a committed Christian and that her Australian husband, the accused, wouldn't let her go to church, read the Bible or talk about Jesus. As a result their marriage had started to fall apart. The murdered woman's mother used to read the Bible and pray with her daughter over the phone from the Philippines when her husband was out. The parents had hoped the husband would someday come to believe in Jesus. When Gary explained what had happened in the interview room on Christmas Day, they began to cry with joy, clap and displayed their happiness over the fact their son in law had become a committed Christian. They had prayed for him every day since the marriage. The victim's father believed his daughter was in heaven and now his son in law would also be there one day. He commented that God can change one very bad incident into one that glorifies Him. Gary was amazed how Christians react to situations of loss, like this family with real faith and trust in God. Even though this death was sad and a tragedy, God used it. Once again, Gary had witnessed the power of God who can take our messes and transform our lives by His will. All messed up lives can be created anew if only people would come to God who created them.

Gary said, "Who we worship and our destination for eternity are the biggest issues to be decided by every person in their own lifetime. Much before it's too late."

- CHAPTER THREE -

THE HUMAN TOUCH

$\backsim$

"Humanity is just a work in Progress."
(*Tennessee Williams, Writer)*

"Racket in the Cell"

For me, anytime in a police cell would not be the right time. Being confined and with my freedom cut off, would be too much for me. I can understand a man getting upset when he found himself shut up in a cell. So it was when police at Blacktown were having a tough time with a non compliant prisoner who was threatening police and harming himself.

Gary had a call from the Custody Sergeant.

"Gary, we've got a fellow down here in the cells and he's out of control. He was arrested for assault, assaulting police and offensive behaviour. Would you help with the cell entry?"

At the time Gary was a Detective Sergeant. He went down to the cell and saw a man with a bald head. Gary later discovered that the man had shaved his head at home the previous night. All his clothes were off. He was running around the cell cursing, swearing, and abusing people. Where possible, police always try negotiation before physical confrontation.

Gary tried calming him because he knew that if the man didn't calm down, they'd have to enter the cell, forcefully deal with him and get him to a medical or psychiatric unit. Standing at the cell opening, Gary spoke to the man. The man spat at him and Gary ducked.

Gary said, "Mate you're hurting emotionally. You're not angry at me or my mates. You're broken-hearted and scared. You're upset because you don't have any hope for the future. You feel helpless and cut off from life itself. This high level of disturbance is understandable and it's all about what you've gone through in the past."

The man replied, "How do you know all these things?"

"I don't, but God the Holy Spirit indicated to me that you're broken hearted and you think no one cares about you. I want you to know I came to tell you God cares for you."

At this the man swore, yelled and said, "God's done nothing for me in the past and I'll rot in hell. I'll never submit to him as long I live. Mother of God I worship Satan!" "Why do you do that? What has he ever done for you except harm you?"

"He gives me a lot of pleasure."

"How long is that going to last?" The Bible says, 'There's pleasure in sin but only for a season' mate. That means there's only pleasure for a short time. A matter of fact, I call it the 'PP' you'll eventually 'Pay for the Party'. It's like a credit card. Spend up big today and you must pay it sooner or later. You need to know God loves you. He died for you in Christ and He wants to give you a reason for living. He paid the debt for you."

Gary moved close to him and said, "I'm not going to talk to you right now mate. I'll speak to the evil spirit in you. Gary looked the man in the eye and quietly said, "Evil spirit you will leave this man and go right now in Jesus' Name".

That's all Gary said. He knew that the Bible says that when Christ is in us by His Holy Spirit, we have power over the enemy. Satan, the deceiver, has already been defeated by Christ's death and resurrection. As a young police officer whilst on traffic point duty, Gary didn't stand up and shout, rant and rave at the traffic. He just put his hand up. The cars stopped and thousands of tonnes of metal obeyed. He was always confident of his authority as a police officer, and he's always been confident of his authority as a Christian as well. Relating this event to me, Gary said that this man went down on his knees when he saw him looking him straight in the eye. He stood up, ran over to the other side of the cell and started to cry.

He asked, "What's happening?"

Gary replied, "Would you please put your clothes on?"

He asked, "Who took them off?"

"You did!"

"I wouldn't do that!"

"Mate just put your clothes back on and what I'm going to do is bring you back out of the cell to another area because I want you to have a shower and clean up."

The man had blood and faeces all over him. He'd slightly injured his head and had grazes which had bled. He didn't need immediate treatment, just a cleanup.

Gary then said, "What we're going to do is make sure you have a shower, and then I'll get an ambulance down here just to check you over. You've been scraping your head on the concrete."

The man said, "I remember doing something like that."

Police officers escorted the man to a shower. He was still crying his eyes out as he was showered. His clothes were placed back on him. Surprisingly they were in reasonable shape. This is not the first or last time Gary dealt with prisoners acting out like this in custody. Some were angry, scared, drugged, drunk or psychotic.

Gary later spoke to the man and said, "I'm going to take you out to the dock area and make you a cup of coffee."

He was given a meal of fish and chips from Mick's shop that had the Prisoner's Meal Contract down the road. The smell wafted through the custody area and made police on duty quite envious.

Gary said, "Look mate. You're the one who's committed those offences and you were drunk and under demonic influence. The Bible says they exist and, if we don't know Jesus, we're vulnerable to the devil. You've got a lengthy record at the police station, but if you believe in Christ, your record will be erased in heaven though not, of course, here on earth."

The man started to cry again.

Gary said, "Do you want to accept Jesus as God's Son who died for you?"

He said, "Yes."

Gary prayed with the man and he went back into the cell and slept 'like a baby'. He organised for the Salvation Army Chaplain to follow up the decision the man had made. The man became a strong Christian. The last Gary heard he was doing well in his new life with God and never offended against the law again.

"Vegemite Lifeline"

A Salvation Army mate of Gary's introduced him to a young man who had certain disabilities and suffered from depression. Gary noted that the young man felt his life was a waste and it wasn't worth living. He had attempted suicide in the past. He had helplessness and hopelessness pervading his life. He was a high risk of suicide according to Gary's experience. Gary gave his mate one of his business cards and told him to give it to this young man and let him know to contact Gary if he was in need. The offer was taken up. Over several weeks, Gary had many talks both face to face and on the phone with this young man.

Late one evening, Gary's phone rang at home.

He answered it with his usual cheery "Hello, Gary Raymond speaking."

There was no response from the other end only background noise. Then Gary heard a slurred voice, followed by a kind of groan and gurgling. It was almost like a tape recorder that had slowed right down.

Gary asked, "Who is it. I can't understand you?"

Still no response only groans and moans.

Gary's first thought was to hang up for he thought it might be someone trying to play a joke on him, a crank call. Then he thought he'd persist with the call, for if someone was playing a joke, he wanted them to think he was either recording it or trying to track the location of the call, acting as a deterrent.

"Can you tell me who you are and what you want?"

More moans, groans, slurred speech and a rattles in the throat. Suddenly, because of his ambulance and rescue squad experience, it dawned on Gary that there was something medically wrong with the person on the other end of the phone. Crank callers usually hang up to avoid detection.

Gary then said, "I don't know who's on the phone, but stay on the phone. Don't hang up whatever you do."

Meanwhile Gary left his phone off the hook and looked for another phone so he could contact the Police Dispatch Centre. They would trace the call to the location. He found one at his neighbour's apartment. All the while Gary tried to think who the caller could be. He continued to talk, but realised the voice at the end of the line was getting fainter and fainter. Gary asked God to help. Suddenly it dawned on him it was a young man his Salvation Army mate had introduced. The young man came to mind and Gary realised he'd probably overdosed because it sounded like that kind of mumble.

After dialling his number with another phone, Gary found the line was engaged. Gary said, "I think I know who you are. I'm getting help."

Gary rang the fellow's cousin, found out the address and got urgent assistance down to the house for the victim. It was a distance from Gary's home so he didn't go himself. Police gained entry into the house and found the young man unconscious and nearly dead. The youth had overdosed on a number of tablets in a suicide attempt and he was taken to hospital by ambulance and placed in emergency, then intensive care.

A week later Gary received a phone call from a nursing sister who said, "This young man you might know has gone on a hunger strike and we're at the end of our rope. It's starting to get quite serious because he won't eat anything. He mentioned your name. He's drinking only water and refuses to eat anything we put before him. He keeps saying he wants to die and that his life is worth nothing. Really Mr Raymond, we've tried everything. If anyone can persuade him to eat it's you. He thinks so much of you because of the help you've given him in the past."

The word of the 'hunger striker' had spread around staff and other patients. Many went to his ward and tried to persuade him but failed.

Gary walked into the hospital, looked at the young man and asked, "Hi mate, how are you?"

"I want to support you. I want you to talk about what's on your mind at the moment." What are you thinking? How you're feeling? How's your body? Why are you acting like this?"

He just couldn't answer Gary for he was so depressed. He couldn't even look Gary in the eye.

Gary spoke to a nursing sister who said, "Mr Raymond if you fail in your attempt to get him to eat, then we'll have to put manacles on his wrists and ankles, tie him to the bed and feed him by placing a tube up his nose and into his stomach. We don't want to do that if we can help it. It's getting desperate".

Gary asked, "What have you been trying to give him?" She said, "All sorts of tempting food and drinks."

With a quizzical look Gary said, "I've got a thought.

Gary remembered one of his favourite foods. Please make a vegemite sandwich for our young friend." Gary walked to his bedside, put the vegemite sandwich down on the bedside table and didn't ask him to eat it but just said grace,

"Father God we thank you for this food, for my mate and we pray for all those who haven't got any food to eat today or can't eat because of injury and disease, in Jesus' name, Amen."

Gary picked up half the vegemite sandwich and started to eat it. The young man hesitantly picked up the other half and started to nibble at it. He started to eat with tears rolling down his cheeks, staring at Gary as he ate.

Gary said, "Well done mate. I'm proud of you. Do you want me to tell the sister that you're eating?"

"Yes that's okay."

"Do you want another vegemite sandwich?

"Yes please."

Gary carried the empty plate out of the room and down the corridor holding it up high. Patients and staff let out a huge roar of 'hurrah' as they clapped his young mate.

Someone said, with a loud voice, "Good on ya mate, we want you to live."

The young man cried, apologised and said he had been very depressed and lonely. He promised to get back on his food and comply with his nurses and counsellor. He still loves vegemite sandwiches and so does Gary. Gary has entertained overseas visitors who don't feel the same enthusiasm as Gary for vegemite! I wonder why? It's thick, black and very salty. Who could refuse that? "

"Certainly not a true Aussie", exclaimed Gary.

"McDonald's, Police Style"

Gary said, "We should appreciate small mercies."

The police had investigated a number of armed robberies around western Sydney and finally found the offender. He was goaled for seven years. Gary Raymond was given an investigation to follow up. Fingerprints had been identified for the same offender involved in a past armed robbery. He had not been interviewed or charged with this particular offence which had just come to light on his prints. He had completed five years of his sentence up to this point. Gary knew where to find this fellow – in Parklea Correctional Centre. Through a Court Order, Gary arranged for the fellow to be taken out of gaol to the police station. During the interview, when confronted with the crime, he confessed that he'd also done that armed robbery.

He said, "As a matter of fact that was the last crime I did before I was caught for the others."

As Gary started to make out the Charge Sheet the prisoner said, "My sentence for this one will probably run concurrently with my sentence for the others."

Gary continued to type up the paperwork.

The prisoner asked, "Mr Raymond who's got the prisoner's meal contract here?" Gary said shaking his head, "Sorry mate, McDonald's, not a gourmet restaurant." Suddenly, the prisoner jumped up off his chair punched the air with his fists above his head and yelled, "Yippee. You bloody beauty. Don't be sorry, I haven't had Macca's for 5 years."

Gary was most surprised and said, "Well if that's the case, I'll get you an upgrade, large fries and a burger with the lot."

The prisoner was so delighted and thanked Gary enthusiastically.

Gary found another prisoner didn't want his McDonald's, and seeing the packet hadn't even been opened, Gary passed it on to his excited Macca's fan who gulped down the second hamburger and fries in a frenzy feed saying,

"I can hardly wait to get out of gaol and be able to go to Macca's every day."

Gary thought, "How we often take the easily obtained things in life for granted."

At least Gary had found a happy customer. One could only hope this particular prisoner turned away from a life of crime when he got out of gaol. Maybe the Macca's was an incentive not to go back? Could be he's out there right now working for Macca's or promoting their products to all and sundry? You never know.

"I hope he doesn't rob them!" Gary said deliberately, but joking.

"To Forgive or Not to Forgive"

The word forgive is hard to understand. Many pray 'The Lord's Prayer' and fail to realise what they're saying when they use the word 'forgive'.

A woman once approached Gary and said, "Will you pray for me? I can't forgive the woman who went off with my husband."

Gary said, "Let me ask you. Have you assaulted or threatened this woman?"

"No".

"Have you damaged any of her property?"

"No."

"Do you curse your ex husband and her or do things to hurt them?"

"No".

"Do you gossip or spread lies about them?"

"No."

"Sounds like you've already forgiven him and the enemy of souls is telling you different. It's not only what we do to people, it's what we don't do that counts as well. That shows we have forgiven them but don't realise it."

Gary believes forgiveness is something we do within ourselves with God's help. The enemy of souls wants us confused. Even as Jesus forgave those who crucified Him, so we should forgive others who hurt us. Forgiveness doesn't stop justice. Justice must still happen.

The truth is we live each day with people hurting or annoying us. We forgive them. In a sinful world that mainly ignores the claims of Christ; we need all the forgiveness we can find. Find it? We can in Christ.

Many people who say the 'The Lord's Prayer' gabble the words without thinking. In reality, it should be called 'The Disciples' Prayer for it was given as a model prayer for Jesus' followers. If people today really understood what they were saying they'd choke on the words, "forgive us our trespasses (sins) as we forgive those who trespass against us". We have to question if we have really forgotten the truth of the words?

Gary is right when he says, "Forgiveness starts and ends with us personally toward people who have hurt us. God is willing to forgive us, so are we willing to forgive others?" Many live with resentment, hate and revengeful thoughts. A number of people actually take the law into their own hands, when all along the Bible says, "Vengeance is mine", says the Lord. The answer is praying to ask God's help and intervention. Giving it up to Him in trust and obedience gives you peace.

"Human Shields"

The shield has long been recognised as an instrument of protection. From earliest times people have tried to create a better shield. Possibly the Romans were the experts in creating the best shields. The shield has been described as, "A piece of armour carried on the arm or in the hand to deflect blows from the head or body."

Interestingly enough the badge worn by the New South Wales Police Force is in the rough shape of a round shield. The Romans used their shields in formation. This made their foot soldiers safe from any arrows that rained down upon them. The united shields protected them. The front line of soldiers used their shields to form a wall. Those behind formed a roof with their shields. As the troops moved forward they were almost impregnable. Sounds like the Police Public Order and Riot Squad!

Gary Raymond is quick to point out our Police Force is to protect us not only from bodily harm but from the many tricks of criminals. The police are there to protect us from crime across the broad spectrum of what might be termed 'devious or dangerous people.' With Gary strongly believing such things, one can understand how shattered he was to discover there were detectives under his command who had broken every rule in the book. Detectives and others who had flagrantly swept aside the sacred oath they had given at the end of their police training. This he sadly discovered when he was sent to command Manly Police Station on the northern suburbs of Sydney. A number of detectives and uniformed police were caught and convicted of taking money from drug dealers as bribes. Operation Florida weeded them out and the court gave them gaol.

In his book, "Take up the Shield" American police officer Tony Miano (a friend of Gary Raymond) was a crime fighter and chaplain in outer Los Angeles and is now an evangelist. Miano is of lighter build. He explained, "I quickly learned while working in the County Jail that the command presence I possessed, and not my physical prowess was what deterred inmates from challenging me physically." Miano says, "It was the authority invested in me which caused inmates to think twice with taking me on in a fight. Good police recognize their physical and tactical limitations and know that the authority they wield is not based on their own physical or mental attributes. They realize there will always be someone bigger, stronger, faster and more cunning than they are. The policeman's strength is delivered from a higher power, the laws of the local, state and federal governments. Without that legal authority the police officer would have no more power than the average citizen or the criminal for that matter."

Gary Raymond totally agrees with his friend Tony. While Miano refers to the American police, Gary believes it also applies equally here.

He says, "The power of the uniform is essential. I quickly discovered this when I graduated and walked out through the gates of the New South Wales Police Academy at Redfern, I soon discovered the power of the uniform, the authority behind it. You can use or misuse that authority." Gary says that in the past, when he arrived at incidents as an ambulance officer, he would be welcomed and admired. However, turning up as a cop he was often insulted, assaulted or told 'where to go' in no uncertain terms. Many don't appreciate what police do for them. Today, even paramedics, doctors and nurses are getting assaulted. It is a shocking new trend.

Gary, whilst on duty, once took a drunk home he found staggering around the streets in the early hours of the morning. The drunk kept abusing him.

Gary said, "You need to wake up to yourself and shut your filthy mouth, I'm doing you a favour, you'll need me one day."

The drunk replied, "I'll never need you as long as my backside points to the ground."

Gary helped him right to the front door of his home. The abuse continued as Gary drove away.

About a month later Gary was patrolling alone in Colo Lane, Blacktown. He heard loud screaming and came across the same drunken man getting a severe beating on the ground from three drunken Pacific Islanders. Gary hurriedly punched one to the ground, capsicum sprayed one and the other ran away. He was later arrested at the Blacktown Railway Station. An ambulance and more police were called. At the Blacktown Hospital the man cried and apologised for insulting Gary the night he was taken home drunk.

He said, "I told you I would never need you, but you were there when I needed you the most. Thank you for not walking away. You put your neck on the line for me. I am indebted to you Mr Raymond, again I'm sorry."

Gary accepted his apology and said with a smile, "I knew you would need me one day, but not this soon!"

Gary said to the man, "You know it's a bit like Jesus mate. We reckon we don't need Him in our lives but when we play up, get into strife or our life falls to bits we soon call on Him. He's there all the time but we ignore Him. He still forgives and helps us. The Bible says that whilst we were yet sinners, Christ died for us."

Gary then prayed with the man and led him to Christ. The man gave up drinking and went to a local church where he is today. He is forever grateful that Gary saved him from the assault but even more grateful, God saved him from the penalty for his sin.

"Before the Man"

When Gary was about four and a half, he was travelling upstairs on a double-decker bus with his mother in Newcastle, New South Wales. The bus suddenly stopped. Adults rushed to the bus windows. There were many cries of, "Oh, no" as people looked at the scene of a crash preventing the bus going any further.

Gary, not to be outdone, sneaked to the back of the bus to see what he could see. He stuck his head out of a half sliding window. He saw that a man had been knocked off his motor bike. Gary still remembers today the man was wearing a brown coloured jacket. There was blood everywhere. The man was unconscious and badly injured. There were no crash helmets in those days. Ambulance and police officers were at the scene and there was a slight drizzle. Gary remembers someone held an umbrella over the injured man but Gary could see under the umbrella. He watched intently as police and ambulance officers worked hard to save the man's life. The scene made an unforgettable impression on Gary's mind.

Gary's mother was busy talking and didn't notice Gary at the back of the bus. When she did, she yelled,

"Gary, come up here, sit and don't look."

But not before Gary had watched the police and ambulance men shift the injured man off the road, place him in the ambulance and allowed the bus to continue on its journey.

When they arrived home,

Gary said to his father, "When I grow up I want to help people who are hurt."

"Where did you get that idea Gary?"

Gary's mother explained the circumstances.

Gary's Dad said gently, "Were you looking?"

"Yes."

"Mum told you not to look. Whenever she tells you that again, please don't look."

With that Gary cried and said, "But the man was hurt."

Gary was confused as to why he was being chastised for looking at a 'hurt' person. Gary settled down but never forgot the images, even to this day. The die was cast. He was being shaped for an incredible calling. Right through his schooling, Gary was right there if a kid fell over. He'd go over and assist. He'd help them up, take them to the school office and watch the teacher do first aid while other kids went on playing. The caring side of Gary Raymond was well and truly evidenced at school. If there was bullying, he'd step right in and want to fight and stand with any who were being bullied. This got him a few bruises. He was also protective of his brothers. He lost a fight once in the playground. A big kid stole his shoes and ripped off the already tatted soles. The soles were thrown back at Gary as a last punishment in his defeat. Even at his first day of high school, some youths grabbed him and cut off his brand new school tie with scissors. He fought them all at once, until the fight was broken up by teachers. It wasn't a good start, but it gained him a reputation. He wasn't picked on again.

When he was about eleven years old, Gary saw an advertisement in a local paper. It called for boys to join the St. John Ambulance Brigade, become cadets and learn First Aid.

Gary was so excited and trembling, said to his mother, "Mum, I want to join the St. John Ambulance Brigade and help people."

"That's fine Gary. I knew something like this would attract you. I'll ask your father."

His mum and dad agreed. His passion to help people could be realised at last. His parents were so proud of him wanting to join St John. Gary's mother chuckled with his father as they reminisced the 'looking at the accident from the bus' episode. Gary signed up and immediately started his first day of training. He was given a first aid kit, a uniform complete with a beret and a white shirt with shoulder patches of the black Maltese cross of St John. Gary was so proud to wear the uniform. As soon as he got it home, he put it on and wore it around the house for an hour or so looking in mirrors. The word 'ambulance' did something to Gary's spirit. Like a destiny or plan. His brother Neil went to the ambulance classes with him. This meant young Gary would be able to attend football matches, agricultural shows and carnivals to render first aid working with a senior ambulance person.

It didn't stop just with him going on duty events with St. John ambulance. Word of his first aid skills spread among the neighbours. As a result, from time to time, people would come running, bang on the front door of their home and in a panic ask,

"Is Gary home?"

"Yes what's wrong?" his mother would say.

The answer would be that someone had been hurt or sick. Immediately Gary would be there with his mother and his first aid kit to look after the patient and wait with them until the ambulance arrived.

The other thing that created a need for Gary's first aid skills was the fact the family lived near a notorious intersection on the corner of Wallarah Road and Hobart Road, New Lambton, where there were occasional collisions. There were no seat belts worn in those days, which caused very serious injuries, both inside the crashed car and when people were catapulted out onto the roadway. Gary's mother became used to him being called out to help, sometimes even in his pyjamas and dressing gown. In the end, because of the calls, Gary's mother kept a couple of rolled up blankets behind the door in her bedroom. She'd chase after her son with blankets under her arm. Gary would treat a casualty and his mother would place blankets over the injured person at Gary's direction. Gary couldn't afford a proper cervical collar like the professionals, so he used a folded up newspaper or clean towel until the ambulance arrived. Some ambulance officers became used to Gary being at incidents around the neighbourhood and once gave him an award for his help. Gary was so proud, and as a young boy, it made a lasting impression on the officers. So Gary at a young age learned to deal with road traumas.

When Gary was about fourteen years old, a male driver was thrown out of an FJ Holden sedan after a collision at the notorious intersection. He was unconscious on his back, bleeding from the ear and nose with noisy laboured breathing. It was clear to Gary he had probably sustained a fracture at the base of his skull which is a very serious injury. Gary confidently dealt with this critically injured man. He looked after his spinal column, put him in the recovery position by 'log rolling' him with bystanders help to drain the blood from inside his skull and airway until the ambulance arrived from Hamilton. The officers asked the crowd who had been looking after the injured man. They pointed to a young Gary which surprised the officers. Before they transported the driver to hospital, they congratulated Gary for saving the man's life and invited him to come and visit Ambulance Headquarters at Hamilton for a tour.

Gary rode his pushbike to Hamilton several times to visit, wishing he was old enough to go out on ambulance calls. Each time an ambulance would leave the station on a call, Gary wanted to be aboard, but couldn't. When Gary was only thirteen years old he performed Cardio Pulmonary Resuscitation on an elderly lady who'd collapsed in a local shop at New Lambton. She recovered. The transporting ambulance officers later told the local paper that Gary had saved her life, a huge responsibility for a young lad. One thing Gary Raymond has never lacked is confidence in his abilities.

When Gary went from ambulance officer to police officer his background skills went with him, and again his first aid skills were the means of saving lives. This was so, especially in the Granville train wreck, where Gary and his team were responsible for saving ten trapped people. This event is remembered once a year at the Bold Street, Granville Railway Bridge and is known as 'The Day of the Roses'. A film has even been made of the amazing rescues at that time with the same name. A new comprehensive documentary by filmmaker Graham McNeice called 'The Train' was aired on the Foxtel History Channel in 2013. Retired ambulance Station Officer Paramedic Barry Gobbe also wrote a comprehensive book on the 1977 Granville Train Disaster called '35 Years of Memories'. He was the first ambulance officer on the scene.

Because Gary was exposed to trauma as a youth, starting with St. John Ambulance duty, he was able to rebound when others were falling to pieces in an emergency. Gary stayed calm and carried on without fuss in critical incidents. At times he was quite stoic and detached. This gave him the ability as the years went on to not only help, but to lead, manage and control people under his direction during such emergencies. There was not a crisis Gary couldn't manage successfully. This still happens even in his retirement years. Solid as a rock, yet having a deep hearted compassion is Gary Raymond. All the while he's thankful to God who gives him the power and strength to overcome his fears. When he's concerned, Gary hands it over to God and doesn't take it back.

"Drugs and Theology Don't Mix"

As a Duty Officer at Cabramatta Police Station, Gary Raymond often left his police car and went on a walkabout to check the street gangs and see who was dealing in drugs. Being on foot, you notice more detail on the streets than being in a car. Gary was in full police uniform. He wanted to see if any member of the Asian 'Five T' gang was involved in drug dealing, extortion or other crimes. Drug dealers liked arcades where they were out of the view of closed circuit television public space cameras. Gary walked down John Street and started to go into the arcade. Then for some unknown reason, he changed his mind and continued towards the railway station. As Gary walked, he saw a young Caucasian fellow in his late twenties. Gary noticed he had a swollen right eye, a blood clotted nose and bleeding upper lip. On seeing Gary, he put his head down and to one side and tried to hide his injuries. He started to walk across the road toward the station away from Gary trying to avoid 'police' contact.

Gary yelled, "Hey come here mate."

The man stopped, turned around and reluctantly walked toward Gary who asked, "What happened to you?"

"I walked into a telegraph pole."

Gary thought, "Oh, here we go again another smart aleck." He nodded his head and said, "Oh, yes a likely story young man. You need to know up front I don't believe in fairy tales, especially yours."

Firstly, what's your name and date of birth?"

Gary took down the man's name and date of birth. Gary examined his injuries. Being a former ambulance and police rescue officer, Gary knew the man had serious facial fractures and said,

"I'm going to get an ambulance, you're going to hospital." Gary called on his radio for an ambulance.

The man anxiously said, "I don't want to go to hospital, I just want to get out of here."

"Come on mate. I'm here to help you must go to hospital with those injuries. You're safe from the gangs with me. Settle down. What really happened," Gary paused, "I mean really happened?"

All the while, the man kept looking around nervously with fear in his eyes.

He finally opened up and said, "I paid a lot of money to a dealer for smack. His mates jumped on me for the money and didn't give me the drugs. I was ripped off. Do they still call it that?"

Gary said, "Yes they do. I'll get some more details. Just sit down before you collapse. What's your address?"

Gary's intention was to check on the police radio to see if the man was wanted or had a criminal history. He gave an address in Newtown.

Gary laughed to himself, but keeping a straight face and said, "Listen carefully, I know this address and it's not yours. I want you to give me your right address. Don't muck me around. If you give me another false address, I'll take the matter further at the police station when you get out of hospital. Do you understand that?"

"Sir, fair dinkum that is my real address."

Gary said sarcastically and smugly, "Well smarty, I happen to know that's Moore Theological College, so let's try again shall we?"

"Sir, that's where I live," the man said convincingly.

Gary's eyes opened wide. He was stunned, "Are you telling me you're a trainee minister?"

"Yes I am."

Gary said slowly with expressiveness, "What are you doing here in drug ridden Cabramatta?" The man put his head down and said, "I used to be a heroin addict, but when I received Christ, my fiancé and I got a call from God to full time Christian service. I went to Moore College to train as a minister, but lately my body has been screaming out for heroin. I couldn't help myself and so here I am an absolute wreck."

Gary said compassionately, "Listen, I know this is definitely not God's plan for your life. You're way off track. You've derailed and you need to get back on track. I'm a Christian police officer and I believe God has supernaturally brought us together today for a good reason and not by chance, so that you can get back into God's will and purpose for your life. When the ambulance gets here, I'll follow you over to Liverpool Hospital for your safety. After your injury treatment, you'll need the Detoxification Unit to wean off the drugs and then rehab."

He said, "Yes, I have to get off these drugs – God's counting on it."

Gary said, "Before the ambulance comes I'm going to pray for you. Keep your eyes open and so will I."

Gary laughing loudly told me that you would never close your eyes in Cabramatta during those dangerous days, even when you prayed! Thankfully Cabramatta is now a great place to live or visit. The gangs were decimated by police in an enforcement operation after John Newman's assassination. Gary placed his hand gently on the man's shoulder and sincerely prayed for him to get back on track for God. The ambulance arrived. Gary had his police car close and was able to follow the ambulance to hospital to brief the doctors. The man went into 'detoxification' after his injuries were treated. He was cleaned up until he was drug free. He went back to his studies at Moore College and graduated with 'flying colours'. In his graduation speech he said he'd been on the streets of Cabramatta and become tangled up with heroin. He said he expected to encounter police in Cabramatta that day, but never in his wildest dreams did he expect to meet God through a police officer in Cabramatta that day.

He said, "That day I was not only arrested by the police, I was arrested by God and stopped in my tracks though a Christian policeman."

The man became a successful Christian minister and has never returned to his old habit. He received total deliverance, with God's help. He is helping many drug addicted people today. How amazing for God to arrange such an encounter. That day Gary was heading down the arcade but looking back, God actually changed his mind and he met a fellow Christian in distress. Gary has never underestimated the command God has over His creation and people. Even though He has given us a free will, He can cause things to happen, or allow things to happen according to His will.

As the song says, "What a Mighty God we serve."

"To Lie or Not to Lie?"
Gary was on night shift, however was required to attend court bleary eyed later in the morning. An offender approached him in the holding cell area and said,

"Can I tell you something? One of your detectives is going to lie in court. I did all the others but not that one."

Apparently the detective was going to allege the offender had committed a crime he hadn't committed. Gary quizzed the offender further. Later, when Gary spoke to the detective, the detective said,

"Well he's done one, he's done the lot. It's his Modus Operandi, it must have been him. He's going to wear it anyway."

He was referring to Break, Enter and Steal offences. Gary moved close and said, "That's not the right thing to do mate. If you drop a load on him, I'll have to do the right thing and tell the prosecutor."

"Oh yeah, good one Gaz. If you do that, I'll lose my job. I'll be on the street and my wife and kids will suffer."

Gary got angry and said, "You have to make this right and withdraw that 'dud' charge. I have no choice but to challenge you on it mate and tell someone if you don't. Don't have a go at me; you shouldn't put either of us in this position. Don't shift the blame to me mate."

Gary went into court. The matter he was dealing with was third on the list so he had to wait. Being so tired from his night shift, Gary dozed up the back of the court in the public bench seats while he was waiting. He didn't take much notice of the evidence being given, but when the prosecutor said there was no evidence to offer on one of the charges; Gary knew the detective must have withdrawn the doubtful charge. Gary's matter didn't take up much time. He returned to the office and enquired about the detective and was told he'd gone home on sick report.

Gary called in to see him on his way home and said, "I just wanted to see how you were mate."

He said, "I dropped that matter and didn't proceed with it. I still reckon he did it, even though there was little evidence."

"How come you dropped it?"

"Well after our conversation, you were sitting at the back of the court with your arms outstretched on the bench seat and head down."

Gary had a beard at that time and was in plain clothes.

He continued, "When I looked at you, the sun was shining through the court's upper window onto you. Gaz for a moment, you reminded me of Jesus Christ dying on the Cross. That convicted me that if I said anything untrue, I'd be wrong at law and in God's sight. I spoke to the prosecutor in the adjournment, and he withdrew it. When I'd finished, I was an emotional mess and signed off sick."

Looking at Gary, with a tear in his eye, the detective with quivering lips said,

"I'm sorry mate; I promise you I'll never do anything like that again. I put us both in an untenable position. I'm glad I made it right with your help. Will you tell Jesus I'm sorry?"

"You can tell Jesus yourself personally. When Jesus died on the cross, He made forgiveness possible. It's not what we've done wrong, but what He's done right."

The detective answered, "I not only nearly jeopardised my job, but my family and my future. I'll never do it again. I was so angry with the arrogant offender at the time." Gary said, "I know mate, but let God and the courts do it all."

The two then prayed together. Over time, the detective and his family became committed Christians. Gary was reminded that justice belongs to God and the Courts, not the police. It's not easy sometimes to see fair justice when some offenders, get light sentences.

"Night Nurses in a Mess"

It was night when a call came through to the Police Rescue Squad. They were needed at a collision on Tavener's Hill, Lewisham. A vehicle carrying four nurses had left the road as they travelled up the hill. Gary attended the scene. The nurses were in a small two door sedan. The back seat passengers seemed fine, just a little shaken. They crawled out of the car fairly easily. The driver and front passenger were shocked and trapped. Gary reached down in the confined space to see what injuries they had and to assess their entrapment. In the dark he could only feel his way. It seemed there was a large amount of blood and tissue down around the feet and ankles indicating serious lower limb injuries. They started to carefully move the seats back in order to get at the injured. By this time cervical collars had been applied to the two injured in the front seats by ambulance officers.

Gary gave a serious injury report to the ambulance officers saying the patients had extruding flesh and probable multiple fractures. They prepared the appropriate equipment to treat the patients once all debris was removed by rescue. Now with a better view, Gary used a torch to survey the injuries further. It was then Gary saw a brown fleshy looking substance around the girl's feet. As he got a better look he realised it was not blood or flesh, but cooked mince meat all mixed up with brown paper and pastry. To his deep embarrassment, it was then Gary realised that the nurses only had minor injuries and no major injuries at all! He was 'caught out' to say the least and had the ambulance people release the wide tourniquets for there was no bleeding. What he thought was flesh was only meat pies!

Looking at the ambulance officers he said, "Sorry guys. It looks like they had meat pies in bags on their laps when they collided. They were returning from the nearby pie shop back to the nurses' quarters."

The rescue and ambulance crews had a good laugh at Gary's expense.

"Love your work," they said to Gary. "Enjoy your next pie. Get the one with smooth red tomato sauce on top Gaz."

A lot more laughter and frivolity continued. Taking the 'Mickey' out of each other was part of the rescue squad camaraderie. It was a good 'stress relief' as well.

Gary told me, "Light heartedness counteracted the heaviness of the rescue tasks." Gary thought, "I'll get them back one day, one at a time". And he did. All his mates had their 'embarrassing moments' which Gary took full advantage of in the mate's 'payback system'.

THE HUMAN TOUCH

CHAPTER FOUR

ANGEL UNAWARE

❧

"This world has angels all too few, and heaven is overflowing."
Samuel Taylor Coleridge, Poet.

"Angel or Policeman"

Gary was at the Police Rescue Squad headquarters in Sydney where a quiet afternoon could never be guaranteed. Weekends kept the squad busy with recreational accidents where people needed rescuing. Rescues involving hang gliders, rock climbers, rock fishermen, vehicle collisions, lost hikers and many more could be on the cards. On this particular Saturday, Gary was taking a break with a cup of coffee when a call came through, "We've got a 'witnessed jump' at The Gap, a notorious suicide spot. Sadly, many people over the years have chosen this spot to end it all. A 'witnessed jump' is where a person is seen to jump by somebody else. A non witnessed jump is where the person is not seen jumping, but their body is discovered on the rocks below or in the water sometime later. Another case may be a fisherman's body washed up on the rocks or someone who'd been rock climbing and fallen.

On their way out to The Gap, Gary and the team went without lights or siren because they had never known a 'witnessed jump' without ending up as a dead body. There was no need to go at breakneck speed for a body recovery, only if someone was alive. On arrival Gary discovered what had happened. A number of Japanese tourists from a tourist group taking photos of the beautiful sandstone cliffs had watched a man get out of a taxi, run up and leap over the safety fence straight to the edge and jump over the cliff. Gary and crew were setting up their cliff rescue machine ready for a descent to recover the body. The cliff rescue machine is like a small swinging derrick like a small crane which has a system of pulleys, ropes and a stretcher which is lowered over the edge with a rescuer.

As they were setting up, a young police officer came up to Gary and said,

"Mr Raymond, I think I saw that bloke down at the bottom move."

Without taking much notice Gary said, "Thanks mate."

In his mind, Gary didn't believe what he'd heard. He reckoned he was a young policeman and people not used to working at heights become mesmerised and tend to see things that aren't there. Gary dismissed his claims as a mistake.

Gary was wearing his white overalls with a light blue climbing helmet, and set up his harness. He was nearly ready for the descent, when suddenly an ambulance officer ran up anxiously and said,

"Gary that bloke down there is alive – I saw him lift up his arm for a second."

Gary questioned, "Are you sure?"

"Sure I'm sure," he insisted.

Gary was more inclined to believe the ambulance officer rather than an inexperienced police officer, but he struggled with the fact that someone was still alive at the bottom. Gary finally came to grips with it and said in a loud voice,

"Let's move it, stat!"

'Stat' is the medical code word for 'hurry up'. Gary's team moved to a heightened level of haste. Gary completed his preparation very quickly, but carefully and abseiled down to the rock platform with a first aid kit where the man was lying on his back. Gary released his rope from the descending device, ran across to the body and discovered a Caucasian man of about thirty five who appeared dead. Gary was kneeling, checking out the man's vital signs, airway, breathing and circulation when to his utter amazement, the man suddenly opened his eyes. Since Gary had been used to picking up dead bodies from this very spot, he was a little shaken at first. Gary started to manage the man's critical injuries, thinking any minute the man would literally die in his arms. Gary again just couldn't believe he was still alive after such a jump! Was it a dream? He was preparing a cervical collar to place around the man's neck when the man opened his eyes again, looked up in a stupor and asked Gary with a soft feeble voice,

"Are you an angel?"

Gary paused to figure out that question. "No, I'm a police officer from the rescue squad."

"No, you must be an angel."

"Sorry, no I'm not an angel."

"But you must be I'm dead."

"No, you're not dead I'm going to help save your life."

The man appeared agitated. "You're telling me lies. I must be dead, I jumped over the cliff. Why are you lying to me? I know you're an angel."

During this time Gary started bandaging his head after immobilising his multiple fractured pelvis and limbs. An Oxy Viva was lowered down for Gary to give him oxygen therapy. Gary still thought the man was going to die.

"Why are you doing that?" he asked.

"You're bleeding."

"Why aren't you telling me that you're an angel? I can't be bleeding, I'm dead?"

Gary at this stage jumped on the radio and called for surf rescue helicopter backup. Then he said, "Look mate, I'm not an angel, I'm a cop. You're not dead and I'm hopefully going to get you to hospital."

With that the fellow got truly upset and started to breathe heavily and cry. He was in a lot of pain.

He kept saying, "I want to die." He tried to push Gary away and said,

"Just let me die. I don't want to live." Gary said, "I can't let you die. I must do everything I can to save your life." Then he looked at Gary with tears in his eyes and said, "Am I really alive?" Gary said, "Yes mate you are." Gary, with a 'straight face' thought, "What a disappointment to expect an angel and instead get a cop."

In telling the story, Gary told me in a joking manner, "All cops are angels in disguise you know!"

The man whimpered weakly, "Do you mean to say I not only mucked up my life, but mucked up my death too?"

"Listen mate, I don't know what you've done, but I've never seen anyone survive a jump over here, ever. I want to tell you I'm a Christian cop and this is a miracle that you have survived. God must have an incredible plan for your life."

Those words would have later significance.

Gary continued, "As a matter of fact I'm going to pray right now not only that you'll live, but also that you'll find God's purpose, peace and forgiveness in your life.

The man crying whimpered, "Go ahead I've got nothing else left."

As Gary, full of compassion, said a simple prayer, his words were soon drowned out by the whirling sound of the hovering surf rescue chopper's blades overhead. The medical team dealt with the man and placed him on board the helicopter and it left for a mercy dash to the nearest hospital. Gary was then lifted back up to the top of the cliff by rope and they returned to police rescue headquarters ready for the next call.

About a year or so later, Gary was lecturing at the police rescue squad base when he was told there was somebody to see him downstairs. He went down and a thin fellow was there standing in a walking frame with obvious limb deformities.

Gary said, "Hello, how can I help sir?"

He said, "You should know me."

Gary was embarrassed.

Trying to save face, he said, "I'm sorry sir, I don't recognise you and I don't remember where we met." Did I rescue you from somewhere?"

The man said kindly but forcefully, "You should remember me. You're my angel!" Gary suddenly remembered and said with surprise, "You're the bloke that jumped at The Gap. Wow, I can assure you, you look better than you did that day. To be frank, I didn't think you'd live, let alone come to visit. Come in." Gary took him into the rescue squad meal room for a cup of tea.

The man said, "Let me tell you what happened. I was a merchant banker in Sydney, being paid a million dollars a year and I started pursuing a prostitute. I fell in love with her even though I was married with two kids. I left my wife and kids for her. This prostitute became my girlfriend. I set her up in a luxury unit overlooking Sydney Harbour. I started to live with her. I gave her a large amount of money and even gave her access to my bank account. One day it came to an end. I came home to discover she was gone. The unit was cleaned out and my bank account was cleaned out. She'd taken the lot without a trace. She probably went back overseas. I lived alone for a while and became extremely depressed. I finally went home and asked my wife if she'd have me back.

She said to me, "No, I'll never have you back. I can't trust you as far as I could throw you."

I nosedived into deep depression, guilt and regret. I got into a taxi, went to The Gap, ran from the taxi and without hesitation, jumped straight over the cliff. I just wanted to end the pain."

Looking back, Gary points out, that because the man didn't look where he was jumping, he fell first of all onto three or four small rocky and vegetation covered ledges. These 'broke' his fall so he virtually had three or four separate falls before he landed at the base of the cliff. If he'd looked to either side of where he had jumped, he'd have had a straight vertical fall to the rocks below and would have definitely been killed on the rocks or in the water.

Looking at the fellow Gary said. "You should have been killed. It's a miracle you lived."

The man then said, "By the way, I do remember you prayed for me at the bottom of The Gap. I've got some good news for you. I've come to Christ, confessed my sin and committed my life to Him and never been happier."

"Wow that's great. How did that happen?"

The man continued his story, "While I was in Intensive Care a hospital chaplain came in and said,

"I've looked at your hospital notes. The way you jumped and was saved must be a miracle. God must have an incredible plan for your life?"

I said to him, "Thanks for saying that. You must have been talking to that police rescue bloke Gary Raymond that saved me?"

"No, I've heard of Gary Raymond, but I haven't been talking to him about you. Why?"

"That's what he told me about God's plan when I was lying at the bottom of The Gap."

The Chaplain said, "That's twice you've heard it then. Don't you think God has been trying to tell you something through us?"

I asked what that plan is and the chaplain explained salvation to me and asked that God might show me a new plan for my life through Jesus." Gary smiled as he contemplated the fact that the chaplain used similar words to him. Gary thought how clever God is in the way He brings people to Himself. God is always making Himself known through His word and through His people.

There was another room just off the foyer of the rescue station. The guy looked over, and without warning gave a loud whistle. A lady walked out with two children. What a surprise! They had been hiding in the next room. They walked over to Gary. It was at this stage, that Gary realised the other members of the rescue squad were in on the 'surprise'.

The man said, "Gary this is my wife and children."

The boy was aged about seven and the girl about five. Gary gave the wife and children a kiss on the cheek and said,

"Hello nice to meet you all. Tell me more about what's going on here."

A cup of tea and cake was provided for his wife and they sat down.

The man pointed to his wife and said, "Why don't you tell Gary what happened?"

She said, "Absolutely. I was notified that my husband had jumped over The Gap and was in a critical condition in hospital. I still hated my husband and thought this was just another drama for us all. I didn't want to see him. A couple of my girlfriends were Christians. They went with me to the hospital and outside the hospital operating theatre, they prayed with me. I felt a real need of Christ and became a Christian. It was a Saturday night. The next day being Sunday, I went to church with them. At the service I went forward and made a public profession of my new faith in Christ. Sometime later, my husband also became a Christian after speaking with the hospital chaplain. He was going to tell me he'd become a Christian and I was going to tell him that I'd become a Christian. When we told each other in the hospital what we'd done, we cuddled, cried, prayed together and decided that, in Christ we'd be made over anew and start again. The Bible says when we come to Christ we are a new creation, the old goes and the new comes."

Gary and the rescue squad blokes were overwhelmed by their story of renewal.

At this stage the husband turned to their children, nodded and said,

"Now's the time kids."

At that cue they both walked from their Mum to Gary. The boy grabbed one of Gary's hands, the girl grabbed the other. The boy said,

"Mr Raymond, we're going to pray for you because you prayed for daddy. Thank you Lord for helping Mr Raymond save my daddy's life so he could come home."

Then the little girl prayed, "Thank you God for all the police rescue men."

Gary recalls that everyone in that room had tears in their eyes, especially him. Most of those tough police rescue men were fathers and these two children melted their hearts. Sandwiches were made and everyone talked together. Since then, the husband and wife have gone on trusting in and believing in Christ. They attend church regularly.

As Gary says, "They messed it up, God fixed it up."

As they left the squad, the man looked at Gary and said,

"Gary, I know you're not a real angel, but you'll always be my angel."

Gary gave a smile and nodded.

Gary said, "That's fine by me."

Gary contemplated, "It's great to be a cop in the rescue squad on days like this."

That's the story of one tough, yet soft hearted cop who became an angel unaware. Had the merchant banker thought to turn to the book of Proverbs, he might have saved himself and everybody else a great deal of trouble. *"For the lips of an adulterous drip honey. And her speech is smoother than oil, but in the end she is bitter as gall." "For the prostitute reduces you to a loaf of bread, and the adulteress preys upon your very life."*

(Proverbs 5:3-4 and Proverbs 6: 26 NIV)

However, as has been said elsewhere in this series of stories, life cannot be lived on 'if only'.

"Peter and the Train"

One afternoon a youth by the name of Peter thought he had a good reason for suicide. Both of his parents had died within a short space of time. Fortunately however, Gary Raymond was on duty driving around Blacktown in his police vehicle. Suddenly two street kids came running up to him. They were hysterical, but one of them managed to gasp out,

"Quick Mr Raymond, Peter is going to jump under a train."

Gary was known to the street kids because he worked on a Christian Street Team and a Drug Arm Team when off duty. As a result, there was a good respect for Gary by the people on the streets. Also they knew he'd help even if he was on or off duty. Gary asked anxiously,

"Where is he?"

"He's up on a fence over there and he says he's going to jump under the next train. We tried to stop him but he kicked us."

"Show me where he is?"

The kids took Gary to a spot near Blacktown Railway Station. Gary saw Peter sitting on a fence above the railway line. He screamed out,

"Peter, come down off the fence now. Don't do this. Don't jump, you'll get killed!"

By this time Gary was standing just below Peter and a goods train was thundering in. Peter stated to push his body up off the fence and prepared to jump in front of the train or between the coal wagons. Gary urgently jumped forward and upward, grabbing hold of Peter's clothing and trying to hold him there. Peter struggled and yelled,

"Let me die. Let me go. Leave me alone. Let me go!"

Gary knew holding him wouldn't work, so Gary pulled his clothes and tried to get him off the fence. Even as Gary pleaded with him, Peter started to hit him on the head and face with a backhanded closed fist and yelled many times,

"Let me go."

Peter was a big young man and had a powerful punch. Gary put his head down to protect his face and was being hit on the back of his head by Peter. Gary yelled over the noise of the train,

"Peter, let me pull you off the fence. Let go now!"

Peter cried out again, "No. Let me die."

Peter's clothing ripped, buttons popped and his belt loosened. He tried to pull sideways and throw himself off the fence between the carriages of the coal train as they noisily rumbled below. Gary couldn't even call for assistance on his radio as both hands were desperately holding Peter. Worse still, he was losing his grip as he again yelled,

"Don't do it Peter. Stop it now!"

Peter continued to hit Gary. It really hurt. Gary was at a distinct disadvantage since Peter was above him and Gary had to reach up. By this time Gary was gritting his teeth. He couldn't let go to get a better grip as Peter might jump. Gary's arms were getting tired. It was a serious struggle. His head was aching after the punches.

Gary prayed sincerely, "God please help me pull Peter off the fence."

Gary grunted then pulled down hard with every bit of his strength he had left in his body, and to his relief, was able to pull Peter down off the fence. Gary ended up on the ground. Gary then realised he'd not only pulled Peter down but pulled the fence down as well! Both were on top of him. Gary didn't let Peter out of his grasp and managed to slip out from under the collapsed fence. He heard the last train wagon rattle into the distance. After a further struggle, he dragged Peter clear. Gary put Peter in a wrist lock and marched him across the road away from the railway track and called on his police radio giving them the full situation regarding the railway fence being down. Gary was exhausted as he marched Peter into a shop alcove and pushed him to the ground.

He said, "Peter stay where you are. What's wrong with you? Why do you want to kill yourself?" Both were puffing for breath.

Peter yelled, cried and said, "My father died and I want him back, I miss him."

With that Peter stood up and put his fists up and was showing his teeth whilst growling and puffing. With glazed eyes he said,

"You won't stop me killing myself."

Gary replied, "Peter you don't need to do this. Your life is too precious. Put your fists down now."

Gary did something he'd never done before or since, either in the force or out of it. Gary put his hands behind his back and said,

"Okay Peter if you're really angry with me for saving your life today, you go ahead and hit me."

Gary gritted his teeth, held his breath and braced for the coming punches. Peter continued to yell and cry and said,

"If I hit you, you'll knock me out, 'cause you know how to fight."

"I promise I won't hit you Peter."

"If I hit you, you'll arrest me for bashing a cop."

"Peter, I promise I won't arrest you for hitting me."

With that Peter yelled with tears flowing down his face,

"Can't you see I want my dad back or I want to be with him?"

A large crowd of onlookers had gathered to watch the 'standoff.' With tears in his eyes Gary said quietly,

"Pete, you're not really angry at me. You've got a broken heart. You're hurting. You're scared. I'm sorry you can't bring your dad back and Pete, I can't take his place, but I can be like a dad to you. Can I help you and support you in these things you're going through? I'm not going to let you kill yourself. You're too special. God has a plan. I'm going to be just like a dad to you. Can I Pete, will you let me?"

With that Peter stared intently at Gary for a long time and said,

"Would you really be like a dad to me?"

"Yes, I really would Peter."

With that Peter dropped his fists. He sobbed, walked towards Gary and Gary hugged him tightly as he said,

"I'll watch over you Pete, like God has been doing all your life."

Gary told me that he saw Peter's tears running down his police leather jacket. Gary heard sirens in the distance. As police arrived, Gary gestured with his thumb up to indicate everything was okay. They called railway emergency crews to fix the fence. Peter agreed to go to the hospital with Gary for a physical and mental health check up. Gary stayed with him at hospital. Peter was discharged from hospital into Gary's care.

Gary kept in constant touch with him. Peter got a job fixing lawn mowers. Over the years, Gary was able to help Peter just like a dad, along with Peter's brothers and sisters. Peter loved the speedway at Parramatta and was nicknamed 'Speedway Pete'. He had an uncanny ability to tell motor mechanics what was wrong with a racing car engine just by listening to it even before they pulled it to bits. He was welcome in the pit area of the speedway. Sadly, Peter died in 2007 as a result of a brain tumour. He'd become a Christian just after Gary's rescue. He had a great influence over many people during his short life. He was always grateful for Gary pulling him off that fence even to the day he died. A couple of days before he died, he told Gary,

"I'll be seeing Jesus soon, I'm not well."

Gary knows where Peter is now, in Heaven.

"On Knocking Teeth Out"

A woman, whilst shopping at Roseland's Shopping Centre, south of Sydney, saw her husband with another woman holding hands and kissing. She was shocked and pushed to despair beyond her coping ability. In her anxiety and sudden grief she contemplated suicide. She went to the roof of the shopping centre and climbed over the car park fence. When the woman threatened to jump someone rang the police. A crowd gathered. A social worker and a pharmacist did their best in talking to the woman. She was highly aroused emotionally, standing outside of the fence holding the railing. She stared at the ground weeping. She refused to speak to anyone. When police arrived they took over negotiating with the woman.

Gary arrived with the Police Rescue Squad. Since he was skilled in suicide crisis negotiation for situations such as this, he took over. By this time, the woman had her heels on the concrete verge of the roof. Her hands were barely holding onto the railing. Gary approached the lady very slowly and carefully. After some careful coaxing from Gary, she said she saw her husband downstairs with another woman. This was too much to bear. She felt helpless, hopeless and let down. After half an hour she seemed to settle down and became happy. Gary knew this was an extremely dangerous sign. A decision had been made in her mind to jump. Gary sensed she was close to suicide. Gary knew people show a false calm and may even become happy when they make the final decision.

So Gary asked, "Have you decided to suicide?"

"Yes," She whimpered.

"Please don't do that. Please come back over the railing?"

Suddenly, the woman started to breathe heavily, let go of the rail and leant forward. Knowing from experience that some people don't jump but rather lean forward and fall, Gary could see what was going to happen. With tremendous speed and strength, Gary ran alongside the railing, jumped on the top of it and slid towards the woman. He swung his arm hard across the woman's chest just before she fell with such force that it knocked her backwards over the railing and onto the concrete. Gary slid off the rail on top of her and restrained her. Other rescue squad police ran forward to assist.

The woman breathless, crying and coughing, didn't stop struggling but yelled,

"Why did you stop me? I can't stand to live, oh no you stopped me. Why, why, why?" Gary said quietly, "It's because I care for you and God knows you're hurt. You're special. You'll see how many other people care for you."

With that, the social worker came forward and cuddled the woman. Then the woman said to Gary,

"You knocked my false teeth out when you knocked me over. They dropped down there." The social worker joined in, looked at Gary and said angrily,

"How dare you knock this lady's teeth out? You get down there and get them."

How strange. There's a story of an Englishman who saved a boy from drowning. When he handed the boy back to his mother she said,

"Where's his cap?"

Gary sent a constable to find the false teeth. They were found intact. The social worker apologised to Gary and in tears said,

"I'm sorry I reacted towards you like that, I was so stressed I've never seen anything like police rescue before. You acted so fast and strongly I got a shock. You saved her life, thank you so much".

She gave Gary a peck on the cheek. Gary realised critical incident stress takes people beyond their capacity to cope sometimes. The suicidal lady was taken away by ambulance with a police escort to hospital for assessment and support.

A few weeks later, Gary was asked by a doctor to visit a mental health facility at the hospital. The woman from the rooftop of the shopping centre was there. She hugged and kissed Gary. They had a coffee and lengthy conversation about her circumstances. She even thanked him for 'knocking her teeth out'.

She said, "I can live without teeth, but I would have died with my teeth if it wasn't for you Gary."

Even though it was necessary to save a life, Gary doesn't like hitting women. But that's what policing is. Doing a lot of things you don't want to, but have to.

She said, "You were like a freight train. I was going to jump. I don't know what hit me. Thank you for saving my life. I have a brand new chance at life now. I'm slowly recovering and am coming to grips with my husband's infidelity and marriage breakup."

Gary spoke to her about God and what Jesus did on the cross for her. He then prayed and thanked God for being there and giving him the ability to save the woman's life. The lady cried and said she wanted to go back to church. Like many people, she hadn't been for a while and had given up on God, although He had never given up on her. She agreed with Gary that God had a plan.

"Death in Pyjamas"

This is one of Gary's most disturbing memories. When recounting it to me, he was emotional.

A call came through to the rescue crew saying a woman had jumped under a train at Newtown railway station, a Sydney suburb. Gary and his rescue crew drove to the station. Station employees had cleared the platform of people where an electric train stood. Gary spoke to a uniformed sergeant, who said,

"Gary, it looks like someone jumped under a train and we're waiting for you to recover the body."

Before the young woman jumped, the driver of the train was carrying out his normal duties, ensuring his train would glide through the next station which was Newtown. Without warning, and to his horror, he watched a young woman jump in front of his train. He would have been somewhat stunned at first, but quick thinking on his behalf brought the train to a standstill. He knew his job carried the risk of this happening. It took many months for him to shake away the image of that young woman as she jumped and he knew he could do nothing to save her. He had to accept it and yet he wondered if it was possible to stop such a thing happening. He knew suicide sadly is a part of life, especially in a city like Sydney.

Gary and his mate got out a Stokes Litter, a basket stretcher, and a body bag that zips up in the middle to collect and carry the human remains. Gary always made it a habit not to go on a railway track until he was sure it was safe. The train's roof electrical arms were lowered and disconnected from the overhead wires. That was done with Gary carefully watching. He didn't want to end up another victim under a train. Gary and his mate put on their surgical gloves, crawled under the train and picked up the pieces of the dismembered body. It was a horrible mess. It was a very unpleasant and challenging task for any police officer......but that's part of police work Gary signed up to. Gary looked at his partner and said,

"Obviously it's a female, but this material from the body looks like pyjama material. What time did she get here?"

His partner said, "Someone said she got to the station at about seven o'clock."

"That's interesting. I'll investigate that further."

They picked up seven body parts, put them into the body bag, zipped it up and lifted it onto the litter. An ambulance took it to hospital where life had to be pronounced extinct. It was transported to the city morgue for post mortem by a pathologist for the coroner.

Gary then spoke to one of the railway workers and said,

"She appears to be wearing pyjamas?"

"Yes, I think she was."

"What was she doing?"

"Oh well she arrived on the platform about seven o'clock this morning and sat on the seat at the end of the platform. I think she was crying. At about nine o'clock she just got up and jumped in front of a train as it approached the platform."

"Hang on a minute mate. Let me run this by you again. From what you've told me, this young lady was sitting on a city bound platform at Newtown railway station, during peak hour in her pyjamas crying. Didn't you or anyone approach her?"

"No. I didn't want to interfere with her, just minded my own business".

"Did anyone approach her? Did anyone come and tell you there was a woman down there in pyjamas with everyone else dressed for work? You didn't call the police or the ambulance to check her out?"

"Nope."

"Okay thanks. I'll talk to the uniformed police and they'll get a statement from you."

Gary went back to the rescue station stunned, saying to himself,

"I can't believe that in this city of Sydney, a young lady dressed in pyjamas could be sitting on a railway station platform in peak hour crying and no one went up to her to ask what was wrong? At least if they weren't willing to approach her, they didn't call in someone else to check her out?"

This incident made Gary very angry and resentful that people would be so busy going about their morning business that they would have ignored this young lady. To this day, Gary is in disbelief that this could happen.

People's dead bodies have been found in units and houses where they've been for weeks on end without being discovered. Nothing surprises him anymore. Many vulnerable people left to die alone.

Gary says, "It's all about caring and going out of your way. In the Bible it states the Good Samaritan 'crossed the road' to care for the man who had been robbed and beaten. The level of community awareness of depression and anxiety has to be lifted and converted into action. We train people how to work, how to budget, how to drive, how to swim, how to garden, how to play sport, how to entertain and much more. We send them to university to learn, yet we fail to train them to help and support vulnerable human beings who may even be next door."

Gary believes that if someone had cared enough to approach and care for the young woman on the station that morning, until arrival of police or ambulance, she would be alive today. A lack of caring and attention was 'the straw that broke the camel's back'. Who knows what that young lady could have been if 'rescued' in her hour of need?"

"Stop at the Top"

"Suicide is a permanent solution to a temporary problem", says Gary Raymond who was a Suicide Crisis Negotiator in the Police Rescue Squad for ten years.

He added, "Suicide is the forever decision." "Earthly life has no rewind button, just forward or stop. Suicide is a premature stop button."

Gary and the Police Rescue Squad often responded to suicide locations such as the famous coastal cliff named The Gap, Sydney Harbour Bridge, towers, roofs, gaols, schools, hospitals or city skyscrapers on many occasions attempting to literally talk people back from the edge sometimes for hours day and night. This gave Gary and the Police Rescue Squad vast experience in suicide crisis negotiation not only at heights, but other suicide methods as well. They are world leaders in this life saving task.

Gary said, "If we got there before they jumped, we had good success in retrieving them alive. People were ambivalent, this means undecided whether to jump or not. If they had decided to do it, they would be dead at the bottom, and if they decided not to, they would be at home watching TV. Most rescues were done by verbal negotiation, but on some occasions we had to jump on people, grab and wrestle them before they attempted to jump, saving their life. Some were standing or sitting on a dangerous loose rock ledge, window sill, slippery roof or a narrow girder and accidently fell over instead of jumping. Others had weapons or hazardous materials to intimidate the police. I even had to negotiate couples holding hands threatening to jump."

Australia has a problem. Each day at least 5 people die from suicide. Each day at least one hundred people attempt suicide. Teenage suicide has trebled in the last thirty years, but is starting to level out. More than two thousand people die by suicide each year in Australia. That's the size of some country towns lost every year. More people have suicided than have been killed in motor vehicle collisions. Males are five times more likely to suicide than females. There is a higher youth suicide rate in the rural areas than in the urban areas. Males under twenty five years old have a high suicide rate. Rates of suicide amongst our indigenous people are proportionately higher than the rest of the population. Rates of suicide for males sixty years old and over are rising sharply, especially if they are living alone. Gary has also negotiated with people threatening to stab, cut, hang or burn themselves, take poisons or using many other methods of suicide. When explosives, guns, bow & arrows or spears are involved, the rescue squad take cover and the State Protection Group is called in. It is a 'self siege' situation and highly dangerous to others near the scene with a risk of being shot, injured by ricocheting bullets or flying shrapnel sometimes, human bone.

The community should become 'suicide prevention aware' and keep an eye on high risk groups. People must be ready to help vulnerable individuals through a crisis causing depression, anxiety or both. A more in depth consideration of suicide prevention by Gary can be read in the Appendix of this book.

CHAPTER FIVE

ALL CREATURES GREAT & SMALL

❧

"We call them dumb animals and so they are, for they cannot tell us how they feel, but they do not suffer less because they have no words." *Anna Sewell, Novelist.*

"Who Doesn't Know an Elephant?"

It's been said a policeman's lot is a 'mixed bag'. Certainly it was on this day. It was a most unusual event and Gary found his police experience widened. An unusual call came over the police radio. Not "one of our elephants is missing" but "an elephant has fallen off the back of a truck."

In his wildest dreams Gary could not have imagined such a thing happening. Since Gary and his mates at first thought it was a hoax, they took their time getting to the scene. After all, who'd ever heard of an elephant falling off a truck – in Sydney of all places? The first general duties police arrived. Imagine their surprise when they found out it was no hoax. They saw an elephant lying on its side where it had fallen. The task was too difficult for two general duty police. A call went out to the rescue squad. Gary had heard of things falling off the back of trucks before, but this was the biggest thing he had ever known! Being a former ambulance officer, Gary wondered how to resuscitate an elephant that stops breathing. Would it be mouth to trunk, mouth to mouth or trunk to mouth? Gary's mind boggled. The semi trailer carrying the elephant had swerved to avoid a collision;

jack knifed and caused the elephant to fall off the truck, breaking the chain around its leg.

Gary went over to the elephant and examined the situation. Using his background knowledge of 'human' anatomy and physiology training, Gary discovered a big lump on the elephant's head, and what looked like a big lump on its hip. It seemed as if it had dislocated its hip. Further Gary noticed abrasions on one of its ears. A call was made to get a Veterinary Surgeon specialising in elephants from Sydney's Taronga Park Zoo to the scene. When the vet arrived, he walked over to the elephant, but was interrupted. Gary, sprouting his medical knowledge, was quick to brief the vet of the situation and to tell him what had happened along with his diagnostic findings.

"The elephant has fallen off the truck and it has a great bump on his head. I think he's dislocated his hip and he has abrasions on one of his ears", Gary proudly reported.

Gary was proud of his diagnosis. When he'd finished, the vet examined the elephant, turned to Gary and said,

"Firstly Gary, it's a 'she', not a 'he'. The bump on her head is normal and the hip configuration is also normal on a female elephant of this species. Yes, you are absolutely right about the ear abrasions. She has some."

Gary was somewhat embarrassed, nodded his head and said nothing. After all, to be fair, in ambulance training school and police academy, no one had taught Gary the difference between a male and female elephants! The vet then said,

"All we need is some antibiotic powder on her ear abrasions."

With her trainer, the vet helped the elephant up on her feet. He got a large container of white antibiotic powder and spread it all over the elephant's ear. The vet stepped a good distance backwards. Suddenly, with Gary in close proximity, the elephant shook her head vigorously. Gary found himself engrossed in a white cloud covered from head to foot in antibiotic powder. The vet, police and everyone roared with laughter at Gary's expense. The vet yelled out,

"Boy, you'll never have another pimple as long as you live with all that powder on you."

Gary gave him and the others a smirk as he brushed the powder off himself and thought, "I hope I get you in a rescue 'Mr vet'. There might be some payback."

The vet was right. Gary never had another pimple and the elephant recovered and was transported as normal.

"The Red Bellied Black Snake"

One day Gary was performing duty with the police helicopter looking for sharks in or around beach swimming areas. The wash from the rotor blades hovering low, sometimes chased sharks out to sea. On the way back to the airport, a call came through that an escaped prisoner had carjacked a vehicle near the Emu Plains Prison Farm and was being chased by police. The police pursuit ended on the eastern side of the highway at the edge of the Nepean River.

Watching from the helicopter, Gary saw the prisoner get out of the car, run to the water, swim across the river to the western side and scurry under Lantana bushes. By this time, the Police Dog Squad had arrived. It was agreed that the helicopter would pick up the dog handler with the dog and drop them on the other side of the river to recapture the prisoner. They dropped the handler and the dog as planned and circled above. Gary couldn't see the prisoner through the thick Lantana cover, but knew he was trapped there and hadn't emerged from his hiding place.

After warning the prisoner of the police dog, the handler set the dog loose and it went under the Lantana bushes after the escapee. Next moment, Gary saw the prisoner and the police dog come scurrying out from under the bushes running for their lives together into the arms of the police dog handler. Gary was puzzled. Looking down, he saw the reason. A big snake had chased the dog and the prisoner out from under the Lantana bushes together down the street. Police roared with laughter, arrested the escapee and placed the police dog safety with its handler for a well earned reward.

The snake turned out to be a Red Bellied Black snake, one of the ten most venomous snakes living in Australia. Not normally very aggressive, however in a bad mood that day under the lantana.

Gary suggested that the NSW Police Force may take up training 'police snakes' given the good job this one did on this occasion, to round up an escapee. He was only joking...well I think he was?

"The Headless Dog"

An old dog was being chased by another dog. The old dog tried to jump over a timber picket fence. When it jumped, its paws became caught between the top of the pickets. It made a big noise. The dog was trapped and in pain on the tip of its toes. Some people tried to get it off the fence but it tried to bite them. People called the Police Rescue Squad. The angry dog had big jaws and was ready to bite Gary. He decided that he'd sneak up behind the dog while others attracted its attention. The idea was that Gary would grab its jaws together and tie a hessian bag over its head temporarily for the rescue which would stop it biting and looking around. Police distracted the dog from the front. Gary sneaked up the rear like a commando ready to ambush. He jumped on the dog and grabbed its jaws together. The dog was yelping, kicking and squirming. As Gary tried to get the bag over the dog's head, a young boy was persistently yelling something out from the crowd.

Gary said impatiently, "What is it son?"

The boy said assertively, "Mister, he's upset because he's got his tongue trapped between his teeth because you're holding his jaws together."

Gary realised why the dog was so upset. He was biting his own tongue, with Gary's help of course. Gary released his grip a little and the dog quickly sucked in his tongue while Gary finally got the bag over its head. The jaws now safe, another rescue policeman used hydraulic spreaders and the dog's paws were released from the fence.

At that moment Gary thought another police officer was holding the dog. He was wrong. No one was holding the dog and it escaped running down the road with the hessian bag still over its head. It ran between parked cars and collided with garbage tins. In a panic, police chased the dog. As they chased after it, an elderly gentleman came walking by looking puzzled and said to Gary,

"Excuse me officer, did you know there's a dog running down the road that's headless?"

The dog had brushed against some bushes, and to the gentleman with very poor eyesight, the dog had no head.

Gary said, "Yes sir, it has a head, but it's in a hessian bag!"

The gentleman looked at Gary strangely and walked on shaking his head with confusion.

Finally they tracked the dog down and put it in the front of the rescue truck until the owner arrived to claim the dog. Gary gingerly took the bag off the dog's head, expecting to be bitten. Instead, the dog wagged its tail with approval and vigorously licked Gary. Well, Gary explained,

"If you were trapped in a fence, had your tongue clamped between your teeth by a big strong burly cop, had your head put in a bag and ran down the road running into things….wouldn't you wag your tail when you were freed? I would."

"The Swearing Cockatoo"

Gary and his mates in the Rescue Squad rescued a Sulphur Crested Cockatoo that had been tangled up in wires. Through the media, they tried to locate the owner, but were unsuccessful. The bird was very shy, probably because it had become scared and was in shock. The squad took the bird back to their depot and called it 'Charlie'. One day a Superintendent of Police, who was to make some presentations, visited the rescue squad with his wife. The superintendent and his wife went up to the cockatoo's cage. The superintendent's wife said in a friendly manner,

"Hello cocky."

The so called 'shy' bird sprung into life and responded with a whole raft of dreadful swear words. No one at the squad had taught him that language. It was its previous owner. The wife asked, "What did he say darling?" Embarrassed her husband replied,

"Oh, nothing darling, he was just welcoming you to the rescue squad."

Away from his wife, the superintendent turned to Gary and said,

"You'd better do one of two things Gary. Train the cockatoo not to swear or give it its marching orders."

"Yes sir", Gary exclaimed.

Next day Gary had a group of trainee nurses from the Royal Prince Alfred Hospital visiting the rescue squad. Gary talked to them upstairs and then took them downstairs to show them equipment in the rescue trucks. Again 'Charlie' came out with a flood of swearing to the friendly ladies. Gary, very embarrassed, tried to explain that he and the staff had not taught the bird those words. It must have been his previous owners. All the nurses said sarcastically, whilst roaring with laughter,

"Sure, that's your story Gary. We believe you, thousands wouldn't."

Then he said the bird would be going to alternative accommodation, although it never did. After all, despite his 'foul beak' he was part of the rescue squad family. He just had to be quarantined from visitors. Charlie also mimicked the phone call bell which often caused the squad members to lift up a phone with only a dial tone. Caught by the cocky again! The Police Rescue and Bomb Disposal Squad still keep up the tradition today with a number of pet cockatoos at their base. All the birds are eloquent in their clean language this day and age. We hope.

"The Growling Doberman"

A man was murdered at Petersham, an inner Sydney suburb. He was stabbed in the street. As the offender ran away, he was seen to throw a knife over a fence into a car sales yard. The knife had to be retrieved for evidence. An aggressive black Doberman guard dog was in the yard and it kept banging its head against the wire fence. There was no one around to let the general duty police into the yard so they called in the rescue squad. When they arrived, they discovered the Doberman sniffing around the knife. Fortunately it didn't lick the blade, so evidence was preserved for now.

As Gary approached the dog from outside the fence, it growled and barked. Gary wondered how he could get the knife. In those days there was no capsicum spray only 'dog catching poles' on the rescue truck. This wasn't an option. He thought of shooting near the dog or up in the air to scare it away. Both actions were strictly against regulations and dangerous of course. They tried pet food but the dog wasn't interested. Next Gary tried to get someone to distract the dog or hopefully get his hand through the fence and onto the collar to tie up the dog up. The dog was too smart for that.

Gary finally put a ladder up against the barbed wire fence and placed some hessian bags over the barbed wire. He then put another ladder on the car yard side. He climbed the first ladder and started to descend into the car yard on the second. As he descended, he had his back to the ladder intently watching the dog. Meanwhile, the Doberman started to become even more aggressive. Suddenly Gary's feet accidently slipped off the rungs of the ladder and he started to slide down the ladder on his backside to the ground.

He regained his balance on the ground and was ready to scurry back up the ladder. To his utter surprise, he saw that the dog had crouched down in submission in front of him. The dog probably thought Gary had descended to teach him a lesson. Gary in fright with a very deep voice yelled,

"Get away. Go on, get away."

Suddenly to Gary's astonishment, the big brave guard dog ran for its life and hid under some cars.

Gary yelled out, "Stay."

Gary with eyes locked onto the dog and with gloves on, picked up the knife and put it in a paper bag. The dog moved slightly towards Gary. Gary growled at the dog. The dog just stared at Gary and didn't move. Gary, still eyeballing the dog, climbed slowly back up the ladder and down the other side. The dog then bravely raced over to the fence and again started barking and banging its head on the wire fence. The knife was now safe in the hands of the Scientific (Forensic) Police. The evidence was collected and the murder solved.

Gary as a Christian was reminded by the dog episode of how

Satan tries to intimidate us, but his bark is bigger than his bite, for Christ defeated him when on the cross and rose from the dead. Death was defeated, swallowed up in victory.

"A Plea for Penguins"

On 17th December 2001, the Manly ferry 'Collaroy' ran aground onto the rock platform at Little Manly Point. Gary was in charge of the rescue operation and commanded the scene from a cliff top above where the ferry had run aground. Miraculously, only one female was injured out of the five hundred passengers. Gary directed operations using a portable radio. He was surprised the ferry had come so far out of the water, with its green hull and forward propellers clearly visible. He saw passengers on both decks of the ferry awaiting rescue as an armada of various size boats came from near and far on Sydney Harbour to help evacuate them. Gary saw it as a type of 'Dunkirk.' The safest way to rescue was from the rear of the ferry which was still in the water. Bringing the passengers up the cliff face would be time consuming and dangerous.

During the height of the evacuation, when Gary was at his busiest, a young female wildlife officer approached him and said,

"Excuse me commander; there's a penguin colony not far from here. You need to check them to see if they've been harmed."

Gary sarcastically said, "Thanks for letting me know, but first of all, if you don't mind, I have five hundred people to rescue off the ferry first, in case it sinks. Is that okay?"

"Fine, but the penguins are a protected species and not many people know they're here."

Gary looked quizzically at the young woman. "I know the penguins are important. We will look after them, but first of all I must make sure that all the people on board the ferry are safely evacuated. People are a protected species as well you know!"

The woman moved away. Gary noted the task of a commander in such situations is to see the big picture and make strategic decisions based on priorities. This woman seemed as if she'd be devastated at the loss of penguins, but was unmoved by the fact that people could be injured or lost.

Shortly after that, a well dressed elderly man complete with felt hat and cane approached Gary and said with a plum in the mouth,

"I'm the lawyer for one of the passengers on the ferry. What are you doing for my client? He's on that ferry you know? What happened?"

Gary after a long pause, Gary said, "I was arranging to retrieve your client safely off the ferry with everybody else before I was rudely interrupted by you. Please move back on the other side of the police tape cordoned area. We'll talk later sir. Constable, escort this man behind the tape and don't let him back in."

Gary thought it amazing that litigation was commenced even before the rescue was complete! The passenger rang his lawyer and not the emergency services.

"Talk about priorities", Gary said.

Then Gary's mobile phone rang with a call from the Environmental Protection Agency. They were most concerned about possible fuel and oil leaks into the harbour from the grounded ferry. Gary again said calmly but decisively, "I understand. Would you mind looking after that? You have the resources while I continue to arrange the rescue of five hundred people trapped on the ferry." Gary shook his head.

Gary thought, "Wildlife officers, lawyers, environmental protection officers and police commanders all have their priorities. How different they are?"

Gary was relieved the ferry was wedged on a rock platform. If it had sunk, the result would have been unthinkable. There were another five hundred people waiting at Manly Wharf to board the ferry back to Sydney. I'm so glad the ferry collided with the rocks. There would have been one thousand people involved had it had collided with the Manly Wharf," Gary said, with relief.

The prosecution of the master of that Sydney ferry was dropped. A key witness changed his recollection of the incident. The waterways' authority withdrew its prosecution in the case after receiving legal advice it was no longer worth pursuing. Ferry Master William Martin had pleaded not guilty to negligence over the ferry running aground. Human error was responsible for the grounding after William Martin had left the wheelhouse in the care of the junior helmsman. Since the grounding, Sydney Ferries accepted a recommendation that, at least two qualified people must be inside a ferry wheelhouse at all times.

"On Stepping into a Fish Tank"

A call came through to the Police Rescue Squad saying an elderly woman hadn't been seen for several days. Gary and his team were sent to investigate by doing what's called a 'Police Welfare Check'. It ended up being a case 'from screams to laughter.' After knocking to see if anyone was home and receiving no response, Gary and his mate found that the doors were locked and sealed. One window was open slightly on the side of the building. Gary climbed up a ladder. He turned on the ladder and climbed backwards through the window.

He suddenly felt 'a cold wet sensation' and realised his leg was up to its knee in water. With his body's momentum, he continued to enter the room trough the window. His wet leg accidentally pushed over the fish tank which landed onto the carpet. Goldfish were jumping around and flipping upside down as they scattered over the floor. So did the water, plants, rocks and gravel. Gary in a mad panic to stop them dying, tried to pick them up but they were too slippery.

At that very moment, an unexpected loud scream came from the bedroom. An elderly lady, the owner of the apartment appeared. She screamed constantly and threw a vase at Gary.

He said," It's the police madam, I'm a policeman."

Gary had now proved beyond doubt that the house was not empty and the owner was alive. Gary found out later, she'd been in bed with the flu without telling her family or neighbours. At the top of her voice she yelled,

"Get out of here, I'm calling the police."

Gary was on his knees, on the floor, trying to get hold of the fifteen fish and put them into a jar of water, using a set of food tongs which he'd found in the kitchen.

Gary yelled, "I am the police madam. I came to check on you."

Gary was in rescue squad overalls, not uniform, which made the identification more difficult for the lady. The woman, thinking Gary was an intruder, raced to her kitchen, grabbed a carving knife whilst screaming hysterically and threatening Gary. He easily wrestled the knife from the woman and yelled,

"I am the police madam and we thought you were dead."

By this time Gary had hurriedly opened the front door, allowing other police and ambulance officers to enter and help the lady. She was comforted by ambulance officers whilst police helped Gary collect the fish and put them into the jar of water. They filled the jar with too many fish and all had to be transferred into a bucket to save a 'fish traffic jam' in the jar. Gary, laughing, told me that it was like 'orange soup' in the jar.

At last the lady calmed down and realised that the neighbours and police had simply been concerned about her welfare. Everyone concerned had a good laugh at the antics of one lead footed policeman. Fish tanks are for keeping fish not for policemen's big feet. Gary well knew that had he been aware of the position of the fish tank, he would have entered the unit a little more 'carefully'. In other words, 'look where you leap'. His clumsy act caused distress for the owner and embarrassment for him. Fortunately, Gary and his mates were good fishermen. All of the fish survived their ordeal. The tank and carpet were restored by the famous Police Rescue Squad. They recorded the job as not only a welfare check, but included fifteen animal rescues, just for the record.

"Near Death on a Rope"

A mentally ill woman became psychotic and stabbed a number of people and then barricaded herself in her apartment by pushing a heavy wardrobe and other items of furniture against her front door in King's Cross. Thankfully, all those stabbed survived with minor punctures and cuts. The flat was three floors up. The patrolling police and police rescue squad were called in to arrest this woman who had become very unpredictable and dangerous. After a police reconnaissance, it was decided Gary would abseil down on a rope from the roof to an open front sliding window, enter the apartment through that window and arrest the offender. Gary and his mates had worked this tactic many times in other situations. Gary descended, and as he arrived at the window ledge, he locked off his rope into the descending device on his harness. He carefully waited and listened for movement inside. Nothing was heard. He gently parted the vertical metal venetian blind to see where the woman was located.

Crack! Suddenly without warning, a loud noise came from the blind as a knife was thrust between the verticals just short of Gary's chest and throat. This happened many times and each time the knife was thrust towards him through the blinds, Gary pushed himself backwards or sideways whilst hanging on his rope next to the building. He used his feet to thrust away from the window. Inertia and gravity pulled him back to the window towards the knife, again and again. At this point he only saw a carving knife, hand and arm.

Again without warning, the woman pulled the blind off its mountings into her lounge room. She glared at Gary, frothing at the mouth and, had a glazed look in her eyes. She straddled the window ledge with one leg inside the room and the other hanging outside the building. Leaning out screaming, she tried to cut Gary's rope with the knife. Gary pushed out on his rope, with gravity bringing him back in, time after time.

Gary had to do some quick thinking. He was in dire trouble. If he attempted to descend down the rope or climb up the rope the woman could easily cut the rope or stab him. He'd plummet to his death. Somehow he had to get into the room which was his only hope of survival. He thought seriously about using his police revolver to shoot her as it was beyond doubt a life threatening situation faced him.

It was then he prayed, "Jesus help me, please help me."

He was calm and extremely anxious at the same time if that makes sense? It does for police. He had an idea.

Gary gave a strong push away from the window ledge with his legs. He swung out on the rope as fast and far as he could. Then, swinging back towards the window he lifted his legs straight out and aimed the soles of his police boots in the middle of the woman's face. She straddled the ledge with the knife still clutched in her hand. Gary's boots connected full force into her face. She flew backwards from the ledge onto the lounge room floor with a loud thud and a scream.

Gary jumped into the room and quickly disconnected himself from the rope. He immediately dived onto the woman, forcefully took the knife from her hand and threw it out of the window. He did this as he knew rescue people don't stand below someone working above. It was safe and necessary to get rid of the knife that way. He turned her over, face down on the floor to restrain her. She started screaming, wriggling, spitting and tried to bite Gary. He struggled with her for quite some time. As the result of Gary's kick, blood splattered everywhere from her nose and mouth. Finally, he managed to apply a wrist lock and then handcuffed her. As she kicked and screamed, Gary slid the woman across the floor to the wardrobe which was barricading the door. He held her with one hand and pulled the heavy wardrobe away from the door. He unlocked the door allowing police, ambulance and the mental health team to enter. As they took the woman away, she looked at Gary with her bleeding nose, black eyes and swollen lips. She said in a confused, almost childlike way, "I'm bleeding and sore. Why did you hurt me?"

In a strange way, Gary felt guilty about the injuries he'd inflicted, but knew it was to save her life and his own. It was a drastic action, but necessary. He was normally gentle with women. Gary felt sad he was forced to kick a woman in the face, however when he was on that rope, it was the closest he'd come to shooting someone with his police revolver for a while. He sincerely thanked God it didn't get to that.

About six months later, Gary was on duty at the Police Rescue Squad, when someone said he was wanted at the front counter. To his surprise he saw 'the woman with the knife' whom he'd kicked in the face six months earlier. Warily, he invited her in watching her every move wondering why she had visited. She appeared friendly and talked straight. Over coffee, she said,

"I wanted to come and tell you, I went to hospital and got the right medication and therapy for my mental illness. I was charged with a lot of offences, but the court found I had diminished responsibly, from my out of control mental illness. Thank God the people I stabbed only had minor injuries and are all okay. I have seen them since to apologise. The surgery on my nose was successful as well. I was totally unaware of what happened. I'm a nursing sister and whilst in hospital for our drama, I became a committed Christian. I heard you're a committed Christian. I wanted to meet you and thank you for your amazing effort, at my window that day. I'm sorry for what I put you through."

Gary replied "At the time, I thought you were going to kill me. I had my police revolver and could have justifiably used it. I didn't need to, God saved us both."

She agreed, "I fully understand why you had to kick me in the face. As a matter of fact, you saved my life and yours, so don't feel too bad about it."

She cried and hugged Gary. He responded and hugged her as well. After another coffee, they even had a laugh over some aspects of the situation.

Gary told me, "It was no laughing matter at the time. It's amazing how people can see the funny side of some traumatic events. I suppose that's how police cope. Appropriate humour, 'black humour' as police call it, is sometimes vital to keep an emotional balance on critical incidents."

After a lengthy conversation, Gary said, "Thank you for visiting. It's great to see you have recovered." She left feeling grateful after meeting the man who "kicked her in the face."

Gary felt a weight lifted from his shoulders. Gary was presented with the annual Thiess-Toyota Award for outstanding brave conduct displayed during this incident. Sometimes fish tanks and a wild woman with a knife are just part of a policeman's life! Gary nodded and with a snide laugh said,

"Yes, but I could have done without both of them!"

CHAPTER SIX

MATCHES ON THE MIND

❦

"Courage is the art of being the only one who knows you're scared to death." *Harold Wilson. British Prime Minister.*

"Trapped in a train under a Bridge"

On the morning of 18th January 1977, two young women, Debbie Skow and Erica Watson boarded the 6.09am train from Mount Victoria which was headed for Sydney Central Railway Station, with many other passengers. Both Debbie and Erica boarded at Parramatta Station. Little did they know that within minutes, their lives would hang in the balance?

About the same time Gary Raymond was on duty with the Police Rescue Squad at Redfern in Sydney. He'd arrived as usual at his rescue station, checked the rescue equipment and then made himself and the team a steaming cup of coffee. Gary then settled down for what he hoped would be a quiet day. This was not to be for the emergency 'air horn' went off signalling a rescue call. A train was trapped under a road bridge at Bold Street, Granville a western suburb of Sydney.

At this stage of his career, the most number of people Gary had been involved in rescuing at any one time, had been up to six, mainly in road crashes. This rescue he was about to face was totally different from all the other rescues Gary and his mates had been involved in. This day was different. The wreck of the Sydney bound express train was full of workers and school holiday makers, including Debbie

Skow and Erica Watson. The challenges to face each member of the squad that day, and the next, would test their skills, endurance and courage.

At first it sounded to Gary that a goods train, with a high load, had been caught under the Granville railway bridge. This being the case, there would be a call for heavy lifting equipment to free the train Gary thought. Sadly, this was not the case. As they travelled to the scene, more information came through on the police radio – "some people are injured." This changed the urgency and the rescue truck lights went on. The siren sounded with an alarm. From then on, continued reports made it clear this was no ordinary rescue. It was a passenger train and many people were trapped in the wreck. At this early stage Gary and his team had no idea what they would be dealing with after the results of a collapsed road bridge. They thought maybe train doors had trapped somebody. As they travelled closer, reports came in thick and fast that people were injured in motor vehicles on the top of the collapsed bridge as well as people inside carriages under the bridge. Among those passengers trapped in the wreck under the bridge were Debbie Skow and Eric Watson. Gary told me, "We thought that somehow debris from a train must have flown up to the bridge. It took us about twenty minutes to arrive at the scene. The rescue truck travelled the opposite way to the main traffic, but the Road Traffic Authority, had phased some traffic lights so the crew had green lights some the way."

Upon arrival, the crew realised that the Bold Street road bridge had collapsed right across the train because the train had careered off the track and hit a steel stanchion. At the time the bridge was built, engineers never thought of a train leaving the track and striking its supports. Meanwhile in the wreck below, the injured were getting desperate, and their cries could be heard by the rescue team. It was time for quick action. The first railway carriage had been ripped apart at floor level as the train hit the stanchion and overhead wires. Carriage 2 had gone through without a scratch. However, carriages 3 and 4 were crushed down within a metre or so of the floor. Gary knew this would be no routine rescue operation. Looking back

Gary said, "We could see a large number of police, fire brigade, local traders, ambulance, VRA members and the public arriving. There was a mixture of sounds. There were screams from the injured, although most were quiet and staring into space utterly shocked. Shouts from those giving instructions and the sounds of sirens in the distance from more emergency vehicles coming to the scene permeated the air."

It was later ascertained that there were 213 people injured. Gary's ambulance training came to the fore. Gary's sergeant, the late Bill Fahey, yelled,

"Gaz, we've got a stack of people trapped in carriages under the bridge. I want you to try and get in. Let's know what we've got under the bridge."

Gary told me that's called a reconnaissance. The rescue team moved into action as they took ladders from their truck so they could get down to the train. Gary saw a young retained fireman running toward a woman, who was screaming and said to him advisedly,

"Don't worry about her mate; look after those who aren't screaming."

He then pointed to a man lying unconscious on his back beside the train and said,

"Check his airway and posture, hurry."

Immediate obedience followed. Gary had no idea what he was getting into, but without hesitating, he went into action. As he did so, he was well aware what his sergeant meant. Gain entry, get in there and find out how many people are alive, how many dead and how many trapped. Down he went onto the track on the north eastern side where there was a sort of tunnel formed by the train and the culvert. The side of the train and windows had burst open from the weight of the bridge. Gary and his mates could gain access sideways into the carriages between the bridge girders. They saw an utter mess. Many people were crushed to death forwards in their seats. Gary climbed in over them, through them and beside them to reach those still alive. Somewhere in the mess were the dead and injured and among them Debbie Skow and Erica Watson. It was a race against time.

As Gary worked away pulling debris this way and that, a man working beside him had a blue singlet, blue shorts and thongs. He'd come down from the street early in the disaster to assist. Gary noticed the man had many tattoos and observed these were probably acquired in gaol because of their single blue colour (biro ink) and poor artistic design (cell mates). There were the usual love and hate messages, nudity and weapons, demons and dragons amongst those tattoos. He also had no front teeth, a sign of fighting or prolonged methadone use. While they worked furiously together,

Gary said, "By the look of those tats, you've got a bit of a past mate?" Embarrassed he said, "Yes you picked it in one. I saw you looking at them. In another time and another place we'd probably be in fisticuffs, but here we're working together to help these poor people. Even in this tight situation, it's a pleasure to work with you, even though you're a cop." Gary responded,

"Me too mate. We're on opposite sides, but working together here in this mess today."

They both had a big smile and quickly went vigorously on with the job. The man later left as more rescue teams arrived. Gary sometimes wonders what became of him. It was good to see the 'cop' and the 'crim' working together in harmony with a common aim, injured humanity.

The left hand side of the train had burst open just as if it had been done with a huge can opener. Speed was vital so was caution, not to mention the courage needed for this rescue operation. People with 'Crush Syndrome' were an issue. Gary examined the bodies that surrounded him to see who was dead or alive. As he crawled, wriggled and twisted his way through and past broken people, he found the stench was noticeable. When the train hit the bridge and derailed, some of these people had evidently been standing. The impact had squashed them downwards. It was then as he crawled forward he came across Debbie Skow. He found her squashed on the floor in a ball. She had been standing in the vestibule of the carriage at the time the bridge came down. The debris was pressing her head down onto her chest and Gary thought she was dead, as did an ambulance officer who had crawled past her a few minutes earlier. Her face was purple, her tongue slightly sticking out. As he'd gone through the wreck, Gary had automatically checked the pulse of the bodies he encountered in case they were alive. As he reached Debbie the first thing he did was check her pulse at the carotid artery in the neck. She had a rapid feeble pulse. Gary was amazed. He saw that she was not breathing.

Her airway was mostly blocked due to her head being twisted and compressed onto her chest. Gary then quickly moved his hands toward Debbie's head but, as he did so, he knew he faced a dilemma. If he moved her head the wrong way and she had a neck injury, it may sever her spinal cord. This would either kill her instantly or she would become a quadriplegic. In that tight situation Gary had no choice because she wasn't breathing. He urgently moved one hand to her forehead and the other to the tip of her jaw. In the confined space he lifted and rotated her head backwards with traction and lifted her jaw to open her airway. Gary held his breath, and miraculously Debbie started to breathe. Debbie took a noisy deep breath and started to hyperventilate. As he held her airway open, the breathing started to improve and some of her colour returned. Debbie remained unconscious.

Gary flashed back to a time when one night he dived into water to get two people out of submerged car in a canal. He swam under water until he was almost ready to burst his lungs. He'd wondered what it would be like not to breathe for a long a time.

As Gary medically examined the rest of Debbie's body, he noticed she had multiple bone fractures. One leg was crushed and almost amputated. It was in fact amputated later in hospital. Gary treated the bleeding from that leg with one hand on the blood vessel and kept her airway open with the other. At least one person had a chance of being rescued alive. Debbie started to regain consciousness and moan. Gary had stopped several bleeding spots. Having been an ambulance officer, he always had sterile trauma dressings in his rescue overalls pockets. He also carried a pocket knife and a small pencil torch. Many times his torch had proved useful, even in daylight, for he often ended up in a dark place in a rescue. As for the knife, he often used it to cut rope, seatbelts, clothing, shoelaces and other material during rescues. With Debbie stabilised by a medical team, Gary moved on.

At one point he had to turn around and roll dead bodies over. It took him about five minutes to change direction and get past them. Looking back he says the smell of bodies was strong. Only his rigorous training and experience as an ambulance officer and in the Police Rescue Squad carried him through the ordeal. It was almost like Gary was immune to it.

Gary said, "I always looked at the rescue solutions and the good outcomes, not the problems. You disregard the nasty sights, smells, sounds or touches at the time as unwelcome distractions that you had no choice other than to cope with."

As he crawled along, Gary came across a number of people who were alive but trapped. As he reached the end of the carriage he suddenly got a whiff of a smell that terrified him. Immediately he knew it was Liquid Petroleum Gas which, if ignited, would explode with catastrophic results. At first he was confused. He couldn't work out how gas could be at the scene of an electric train wreck. The colour drained from his face. He knew rescuers would be using things that could create a spark. They didn't know the train was full of gas. This was no place for matches, cigarette lighters, welders, cutters, motors or any other source of a 'spark'. From then on he had 'explosion' on his mind for he knew the whole wreck could blow sky high and blow everyone to 'kingdom come' given the right air/gas mixture. Neither Debbie nor Erica knew how close Gary was as they swung in and out of consciousness. Neither were they aware of their supreme danger.

Gary yelled, "No one ignite a match or use a cigarette lighter. Turn off your torches."

He then turned to the open side of the wreck and yelled again,

"Don't use any rescue gear that creates a spark − we've got LPG under here."

At that moment other rescuers on the western end of the train yelled out they'd also smelt gas. Gary was concerned someone would strike a light or use a 'non gas safe' torch to see in the dark.

When Gary saw heaters on the roof, he realised this was because the train had come from the Blue Mountains, where it's cold first thing in a winter's morning. The heaters had been ripped off the wall by the force of the impact. They were pushed down to the floor. The cylinders remained stored in locked cupboards at the end of each carriage during the summer. The bridge had crushed the cylinders breaking them open. This was the source of gas. Gary knew there could easily be an explosion. This would have been what they call a 'BLEVE' (Boiling Liquid Expanding Vapour Explosion). A 'BLEVE' is extremely dangerous and very powerful. It can occur when a vessel containing pressurised LPG is heated and ruptures. For instance, on Sunday August 10th 2008, a massive explosion levelled the site of a propane facility in Toronto. The fire that resulted, forced 12,500 people from their homes. The blast was so big it sent large storage tanks twice the size of rail cars off their mounts and one ended up five hundred metres away. Due to the presence of gas, Gary could only use his hands, sometimes with gloves, to feel close to the bodies of the injured. His pocketknife was handy. Gary had to find out what was crushing or trapping people before formulating a rescue plan. At least the injured and rescuers were spared the calamity of an explosion. Thankfully, the NSW Fire Brigade, now known as Fire and Rescue NSW, used a huge foam generator fan with a duct, which runs on water from a hose not a motor, to help evacuate the gas 'spark' free.

Gary crawled on. It took him over a half an hour to crawl through the carriages. It was a horror journey as he crawled over the dead; some having been compressed forwards in their seats. As he manoeuvred through the carriage,

Gary asked himself, "Who can I save out of this mess?"

Mess was the right word for it, although he didn't realise his overalls were one mess of blood and other body fluids. One thought filled Gary's mind, "Rescue, rescue, rescue." Two others in the wreck also had the same word on their minds, whenever they drifted back into consciousness.

"You were the rescuer so you just had to do it no matter what. There was no one else, you were it," Gary had said with his head slightly down.

At one stage as he crawled, he was held back. To his discomfort, he discovered he had a small piece of human bowel tangled around his foot. He jerked himself free and went on to find others who were still trapped alive.

It was then he came across Erica Watson. He found out from Erica that she was an accomplished ballerina. As he helped her, he realised she was uncomfortable because a dead body was in the way. Gary rolled the body aside to reach Erica. In order to do this, he had to lie across the deceased.

"It was more tolerable than lying on extremely sharp debris and my aim was to help Erica no matter what," Gary said, apologetically.

He had to take extreme care of himself because the damage caused by the crash meant the seats had bare metal with sharp edges. He didn't want to be injured and become a victim himself. By this time other rescuers had entered the wreck and Gary was able to focus his attention and concentrate on the two women, Debbie and Erica, who were quite close together. Gary and his mates had to work out exactly how to rescue them. He couldn't just take them out of the wreck and he was aware of them suffering from Crush Syndrome. This is where skeletal muscle, especially those attached to legs and arms, are compressed. When the blood circulation to the limb is obstructed, a lack of oxygen causes toxins to be formed and other toxins come from the chemicals out of broken cells. If a person has been trapped for some time and is released too quickly, they can lose blood into that area and they can go into shock. The other danger is that released toxins can run back into the veins, spread through the body and cause either heart irregularities, kidney failure and much more. In the case of both Debbie and Erica, the weight caused by the debris couldn't be lifted off until they were first stabilised by medical teams. Fortunately, Gary was able to get help from doctors, nurses and ambulance officers who gave intravenous treatment and other medications which prepared the trapped people's bodies for delayed release from their train wreck prison. Gary had to make quick decisions in order to save victims. In the poor light and confined hot conditions, he had to do what was practical. He had to know which way to carefully lift a person or clear things that trapped them while not aggravating their injuries, especially spinal injuries. All the while more medical help was arriving at the crash scene. Gary helped the medical workers reach the injured. He moved dead bodies aside with dignity, so that those still alive could be removed from the wreckage.

Meanwhile Debbie Skow was slipping in and out of consciousness. When she was conscious, Gary kept on telling her he'd stay with her until she left the wreck. At the time Gary was a little unsure as to whether or not he'd be able to rescue Debbie alive. During the rescue, Gary was starting to show signs of discomfort. He was dehydrating because he'd been sweating so much. Lying down he couldn't drink, so ambulance officers passed small blocks of ice in paper cups. Gary had to turn his head on the side and pull the side of his cheek open to empty the ice into his mouth. Gary's situation was no picnic – he even had to urinate out of sight under a damaged seat, whilst lying down, because he couldn't get out of the carriage to a toilet. There was no time for Gary to eat and, even if he was able to, there was the risk of infection. Besides, people around him were fighting for their lives. There was no time for self comfort. Ice was enough.

Both Debbie and Erica were just surviving. Because they both needed surgery with anaesthetic it was 'nil by mouth' for them, except for an ice block Gary rubbed on their lips to comfort them. He continued to rescue Debbie who asked lots of questions as she faded in and out of consciousness. She asked about her injuries. At one stage, because she knew she had abdominal injuries, she slowly and faintly asked Gary,

"Do you think I'll ever be able to get married and have a baby?"

Gary wanted to be truthful and he didn't want to say,

"Yes you'll have dozens of them." On the other hand he didn't want to say,

"You may not live, let alone ever have a child."

He answered in what he considered was the only way possible,

"I don't know Debbie, only God knows."

Gary said to me, "Well, there are many things that only God knows. We have to trust Him."

Erica also had questions of Gary. She'd told him she was a ballerina and asked him, "Will I ever dance again?" It was another difficult question for Gary who answered, "I don't know Erica. Let's see what happens after your injuries are treated."

Gary honestly thought, "Lady you're going to be fortunate to stay alive, let alone dance again."

During his time in the wreck, Gary helped several people, but worked mainly with Debbie and Erica because of their critical condition. Gary also made a promise to both ladies when he said,

"When you leave this wreck, I'll leave with you."

This was his way of encouraging them so that they knew, no matter what happened he was going to rescue them. But Gary was not in charge and didn't have all the say. Suddenly, there was a bitter blow.

The late Sergeant Joe Beecroft, the Officer in Charge of the Police Rescue Squad, crawled in and whispered to Gary, so the trapped people couldn't hear,

"Get out from under the bridge, the partially collapsed bridge is becoming very dangerous and shifting."

Gary was not pleased to hear the request. He told Joe he would rather stay.

"Gary, the engineers say the bridge is shifting; get out now otherwise you'll be crushed to death." Joe said. Gary replied whispering,

"But Joe, I've promised these girls I'd stay with them. What if I stay very low in the carriage between the steel girders of the bridge? I should be safe if it comes down further." In a serious gruff quiet tone Joe said,

"Gary, get out NOW."

"But Joe I told the girls that when I left, I'd take them with me. I can't leave them here by themselves in the condition they're in."

"You'll be in the same condition they're in if you stay".

"But Joe I'll stay very low." Joe lost patience, moved closer to Gary and softly barked,

"Stone the flaming crows, suffering warts. Constable Raymond I direct you to get out NOW."

Joe was a committed Christian and didn't swear, but I bet he felt like it on that occasion. Gary was reluctant but replied,

"Coming out now Sergeant."

He knew Joe meant business when he changed his language from 'Gary' to 'Constable'. He changed from a mate, to a boss issuing an official direction. Gary knew it was not the police way to disobey a reasonable direction from a senior officer. It was a Police Regulation offence and Gary could be departmentally charged with disobeying the direct order, if Joe reported it. Putting that aside, Joe was like a father to his men, always leading from the front. He'd never done this before, ever.

Gary told me, "Throughout all of my ambulance and police service I had never left an injured or trapped person and never had to do it again, thank God. It was horrible. It was against my grain. I felt so guilty and in some ways ashamed, although it was necessary at the time."

Obeying the direct order to get out of the wrecked train, Gary crawled backwards because there was no space to turn around. He crawled out between the girders onto the open side of the carriage. He couldn't get the trapped people out of his mind for a second. As he walked along the railway track he realised it was the first time he'd seen daylight for five hours or so. The sunlight was so strong he had to shield his eyes. As he did so he looked down at his overalls. They were covered in massive streaks of blood, soot and grease. Gary looked around and saw hundreds of people. The number of people surprised him. These included members belonging to the police, ambulance, fire, Volunteer Rescue Association, defence force, Salvation Army, clergy, railway, electricity, water, media, and members of the public. He also saw heavy machinery. He was amazed and surprised to discover that while he'd been under the bridge in the wreck, a huge number of rescue resources had arrived. It was as if he had been isolated, in another world under the bridge.

This was back in the days when he was a smoker and beer drinker. While in the wreck he'd forgotten about cigarettes and beer. Suddenly he realised he needed a smoke. Immediately he lit up and was given food and soft drink by the Salvation Army mobile canteen crew. Little did Gary realise, the time would come when the last thing he would want is a smoke and a beer. All of his mates were surprised when he would later give them up. Gary didn't know that down the track, he would join the one's giving him food that day. He was destined to come to Christ and wear Salvation Army uniform.

When Gary asked his sergeant if there were any fresh overalls he was told,

"No, keep the ones you've got on, they'll have to be burnt anyway and we're not going to burn two pairs of overalls."

Gary felt self conscious as people were staring at his filthy and bloodied overalls. It was a sort of picture reflecting the mayhem he had just been through and was just about to go back to. Gary also noticed the railway tracks had been covered with sand and rock ballast so that the ambulances could drive onto the tracks close to the train wreck in order to take away the injured. There were cranes and heavy machinery working away shifting debris. Engineers and railway personnel quickly stabilised the bridge and stopped it slipping any further. This was done by using jacking and cribbing techniques. The railway recovery crews were amazing. A helipad had been set up in a paddock nearby and was being used by Australian Army helicopters. A green style marquee tent was set up as a field mortuary which Gary's brother Neil was working in to identify and photograph bodies.

Meanwhile back in the wreck, both Debbie and Erica wondered where Gary had gone; after all he'd promised he'd get them out. For them every minute seemed like hours. Gary was distressed for he knew he'd promised to come back to get them out. Time seemed to be going too slowly for Gary as he paced up and down the tracks waiting for the green light to return. Finally he asked Joe,

"How long is this going to take?" Joe snapped back,

"It will take as long as it takes. I'll tell you when you can go back in. Just be patient, they're doing their best."

Gary was under orders, but was most unhappy. It took half an hour or so before the bridge was stabilised. As Gary's boss mouthed the order telling his rescue crew to go back into the wreck, Gary was back into the small 'tunnel' formed by the collapsed bridge. He crawled as quickly as he could to get beside the two women he'd left with the pencil torch. Crawling back he at last saw the dim light of the torch. To his relief he found both Debbie and Erica still alive.

"See I told you I'd be back", Gary said choking with emotion, but not revealing his true feelings. Both girls assured Gary they knew he would return.

Gary told me, "That incident reminds me of Jesus' promise to return to rescue us. I hope people don't lose faith and trust that He will come back, at the right time. I'm looking forward to His return, if I don't see Him in heaven first that is."

The rescue process continued, when finally the two young women were taken out of the carriage. No less than ten people had been trapped and it took a full rescue team a whole day to get them all out – indicating how badly injured and trapped they were.

Gary told me, "There was a huge amount of disentangling to get those people out of the wreck. We strapped them onto spinal lifting boards."

As for Debbie and Erica, their moment of rescue finally came. As the two young women were carried away from the wreck, Gary stood and wondered and hoped they'd survive. The question uppermost in his mind at that moment was would they live to see another day. The living had all been rescued out of the wreck. During that night, the bridge was broken up by heavy machinery and removed on semi trailers to a secure site for forensic examination. The next day, the eighty or so dead were removed by Gary's team and carried on canvass stretchers to the mortuary tent. Even though the three

Raymond brothers were on the scene, because of the busyness, they didn't see each other. Gary said he was very proud of all of his brothers, but especially the two who were at Granville with him.

After the body recovery was complete, rescue trucks were re-equipped. A lot of gear was missing, either used by others or stolen. There was a short operational debriefing by the police bosses.

Gary said, "We left and drove to a local hotel for a well earned 'drink', in overalls, before returning to base. Hotel patrons shouted us drinks as we sat on the floor against the wall, exhausted. They gave us a standing ovation for a job well done. Even now when I see a train crash on the news, I feel deeply for the victims and rescue workers alike. I know what they're going to go through."

Some years later, Gary was invited on television for the series 'Where Are They Now.' He entered the studio with lots of lights and an audience, and to his surprise, Debbie was there. They had a tearful reunion and they talked about the Granville disaster. Then there came a complete surprise for Gary. Someone walked onto the set behind Gary nursing a baby. She introduced the baby as Shelby Jacqueline Woodgate. Gary was given the baby to hold. He then found out that Debbie had met her husband Stephen, and against all odds, they were able to have a baby. Debbie said that having her baby was a shock and surprise as doctors had said that, due to her injuries whilst crushed, she wouldn't be able to conceive and carry a child. Gary was amazed, for at the time of the train wreck, he didn't think Debbie would survive, let alone get married and have a baby. He thought back to the moment in the train wreck when Debbie asked if she would be able to get married and have a baby. Gary remembered he said to her,

"Only God knows." Debbie then said,

"God knew Gary. Didn't He?"

Everyone in the studio erupted into tears including tough Gary of course. It reminded Gary that God knows everything about us from conception to eternity. As for Debbie Woodgate, prior to the wreck, the last time she was in church was for Sunday school. A little later Debbie attended church and said of the minister, Michael Robinson,

"I'd never heard such a passionate speaker. I found warmth and friendship. I became a committed Christian."

Debbie and Steve have recently fostered two boys rescued from neglectful situation. They still see Gary and Michelle from time to time remaining good friends.

A couple of years after Granville, Erica Watson, the ballerina, spoke to Gary on the phone. After talking about the disaster and her recovery she said to Gary,

"Guess what I did?"

"No I can't guess. What?" Gary said.

"I received Jesus as my personal Saviour."

"Wow, when was that?"

"On Thursday 29th November 1979." Gary paused and nearly dropped the phone. With awe Gary replied,

"Erica, that's the same day I did the same thing."

It then dawned on Gary and Erica that in 1977, both were together in a train wreck at Granville, one a rescuer and the other a victim, and both with little faith in Christ. Miraculously, on the same day, under different circumstances and different places, God touched their hearts and they both responded.

"That can't be by chance. This is more evidence of God." Gary said.

Erica's daughter has now taken up ballet just like her mum. She is studying at a dance studio in Melbourne. Because of Granville and her injuries, Erica is not dancing anymore with her feet, but is dancing with joy in her heart with what God has done in her life to sustain her. The whole 'Granville' experience made Gary feel vulnerable.

He said, "Here were ordinary people going about their ordinary daily activities and their train unexpectedly came off the rails and hit a bridge support. I lived on the edge every day in rescue work, in the extreme, and survived."

At one of the Granville memorial services held each year, a woman came up to Gary and said,

"Are you Gary Raymond?"

"Yes." The lady kissed him on the cheek, hugged him and said,

"That must have been really awful for you discovering my parents and two children who lost their lives?"

Gary's mind flashed back. He recalled the bodies of an elderly couple in the wreck. When the bodies were lifted, Gary and the rescuers discovered two small children on their laps, sadly also dead. Clearly, the grandparents had tried to shield the children when the train derailed and the bridge was sliding down onto the carriage. Sadly their efforts to save the children and themselves had been of no avail. The lady thought the bodies were badly compressed and torn.

Gary said, "No their bodies were compressed together, but were completely intact. You need to know your parents grabbed them from the opposite seat, put them on their laps and threw themselves over your children in an effort to save their lives." The lady burst into tears and said,

"Thank you, thank you." Her face was covered with tears as she went on to say,

"For years, I've been having intrusive thoughts and nightmares about them all ending up in a mess, but they weren't."

She again thanked Gary for giving her a completely different view of her family that fateful day. She walked slowly away feeling much more at peace with herself and the truth of the disaster.

Gary told me, "It's often beneficial for survivors, survivor's relatives or friends to meet and speak with rescuers. It fills in any missing pieces of information to complete the picture of the rescue. The rescuer is sometimes the last person to see them alive or dead. It's like a jig saw puzzle with missing pieces. This helps the grieving process and stops factual guesswork. Even in deep grief, it gives comfort to have answers to your nagging questions."

Gary doesn't use the word 'closure' anymore.

He says, "Closure doesn't exist, just some days are better than others throughout the lives of those left behind after tragedy. It's often on their minds, which is normal and permissible. If people say, "Forget it", that's irrational, as memories are placed by 'permanent marker' on our brains. They come up from time to time, in varying intensity, and then go away for a while. There is no closure. It is just the way we respond to this grief counts, as we go through life trusting God with the management of these memories."

CHAPTER SEVEN

STRANGE WAYS OF NORMAL (?) PEOPLE

~~◠~~

"To make a start where we are, we must recognize that our world is not normal. But only usual at present."
Dallas Willard, Professor of Philosophy.

"A Very Canny Trick"

A number of Blacktown retail stores in the western suburbs of Sydney, complained about the theft of expensive items. Whilst the stores used CCTV cameras they were still unsuccessful in tracking down the thieves. The stores had even increased the number of Loss Prevention Officers to try and track down the thief or thieves. They operated undercover, but still failed. Drug users had been eliminated as suspects and the number of bag searches had been increased at the exit area of the stores. It was then that Gary suggested they review the CCTV footage with fresh eyes to see if there was something or someone they'd missed. As a result, a number of detectives were given footage to review. On the third day of Gary reviewing a set of the tapes, he saw an elderly lady of Mediterranean appearance carrying a plastic shopping bag containing a large square shaped tin of olive oil. Gary noticed her select a pair of jeans from a fixture and go in to a changing cubicle, draw the curtain and emerge a short time later without the jeans. She was not wearing the jeans and her bag only contained the tin of olive oil. Gary then remembered seeing her on a previous tape the day before. He'd noticed this and so decided to review those tapes again. Reviewing the tapes, he observed the same behaviour. The woman had a shopping bag with only a tin of olive oil. Gary eventually tracked down eight or nine of these occurrences with the same woman, bag and tin. He took the tapes down to the Police Electronics Unit and they were enhanced. When this was done, Gary observed on an enlarged photograph the 'use by date' on the olive oil container was the same on all the containers in the different videos. It was the same tin! A pattern emerged. This woman needed watching as a suspect.

As a result, one Tuesday afternoon Gary went to the manager's office and observed the woman come into the store. They watched her behaviour which was exactly the same as previous occasions. She walked out of the store, but this time Gary was there with one of the store detectives. They asked the woman if she had left the store with anything she hadn't paid for. He looked in her shopping bag; she smiled and pretended not to speak English. She held the shopping bag open willingly and exposed the olive oil tin. Gary noticed the bottom of the bag was not flat but bulky. Gary then cautioned the women and asked her to remove the tin from the bag. As she lifted the tin an expensive pair of jeans fell out from the bottom of the tin! Gary realised the woman had been stealing expensive goods and storing them in the empty olive oil tin through a cutaway opening in the bottom and was able to leave the store without paying! The woman of Greek origin was sixty eight years old, a Blacktown local. She was arrested and charged. By the way, she spoke perfect English.

After receiving information, Gary and his team obtained a Search Warrant from the court and went to the woman's home. During the search, many items of stolen clothing were discovered. This meant even more charges. Her two adult sons were very well dressed. It was estimated she'd stolen $10,000 worth of goods. It was like Aladdin's Cave. She received a six months suspended gaol sentence and was fined $1,000. The goods were returned to their rightful stores. Gary has many stories of sophisticated 'shop lifters' methods.

"These types of thieves are as good as their imagination. Their inventiveness would be great if turned into good," Gary said.

"Bible Cigarettes"

Gary was doing his rounds and came across a woman in custody. As the Duty Officer, doing the rounds was a matter of routine to check the prisoner's security, health, welfare and to ensure they were not suicidal. He said to this woman,

"Is there anything you need?"

"Yeah, I want a Bible."

Gary was delighted and thought that was really nice, so he gave her a Gideon's Bible. There were several Bibles around the police station so people could swear on them when declaring 'the whole truth and nothing but the truth'. Gary thought how lovely this woman wanted a Bible. She may stop her life of crime after all. Sadly, Gary found out later she just wanted thin Bible paper to use for rolling tobacco cigarettes when she got to Silverwater Gaol later that day.

Reflecting on this incident, Gary said he wasn't worried what this woman did, for he'd heard stories of how prisoners had obtained a Bible for the purpose of rolling their own cigarettes and found their lives changed as they started to read the words before their smoke. He never heard what happened in this case, but he just hoped the Bible ended up being used in the right way. Gary is a firm believer in the power of the Bible. It says in *2 Timothy 3:16, "All scripture is God breathed and is useful for teaching, rebuking, correcting and training in righteousness." (NIV)*

Gary often calls the Bible, 'The Police Training Manual' or 'The Police Officer's Safety & Survival Manual'.

"Catching Superman"

Gary was patrolling late one night alone. He was Duty Officer. He noticed some youths fooling around. They were on their way home from a fancy dress party. One was dressed as Superman. It was a very accurate Superman suit, obviously hired. The youths were kicking bins over. Next minute, 'Superman' kicked in a shop window. At this stage they hadn't seen Gary. Gary got out of the police car and after a confrontation and short struggle, wrestled him to the ground and handcuffed him. Someone from the crowd yelled,

"You must be a tough hero; you caught Superman single handed—we're not taking you on"!

Another yelled, "Can you reach the roof of the police station in a single bound?"

Yet another, "You must be carrying kryptonite Mr Raymond."

Gary called a caged truck and took the youth back to the police station and when he walked in, the staff started to laugh raucously. Superman however, wasn't feeling so good after his ride. At one stage he vomited all down his superman suit. Then he used his cloak to wipe the vomit from his face. He even wet his 'tights' leaving a big wet patch in his crutch. It was a bad look for the 'super man'. He was bailed out after being charged with malicious damage and resisting arrest. His fellow 'heroes' took him home.

The story of Gary's catch spread quickly. Next morning when the superintendent arrived at work, someone told him about the incident. He looked at Gary and said,

"Well done. Did you arrest Superman on the ground or in the air Gary?"

He then added, "If I want to increase the staff numbers I'll tell the Commissioner, "No more police required, I have Mr Raymond. I have an officer who can arrest Superman! No need for more police with Gary Raymond here."

Other workmates were making comments like,

"All the shift is going home Mr Raymond, you can look after the patrol alone after what you did to Superman!"

"Are you handing in your gun to carry kryptonite?"

Many more staff had comments directed at Gary, too embarrassing for my book. His reputation followed him. The last Gary saw of Superman, he was staggering down the road between 'Spider Man' and 'Super Woman' on his way home to sleep off his 'super night.'

"Moll Fire"

A call came through to attend a single car collision in the industrial area of Blacktown. A car had mounted a high concrete and soil filled nature strip in the middle of the road. The vehicle had caught fire which was extinguished by the Fire Brigade. On Gary's arrival he noticed the vehicle was stuck on the strip and the front tyre of the vehicle had been spinning uncontrollably, causing friction on the bark and soil. This meant the tyre caught fire before the vehicle. The driver told police another vehicle had run him off the road. As Gary had another look at the vehicle he noticed the front right wheel appeared as if it had been spinning and had dug a hole in the ground. At the scene, a witness approached Gary and said he had seen a female passenger run away from the crashed car and he described her. Gary asked a policeman to find the girl passenger described as thirty years old with thick makeup, puffing a cigarette, wearing an extremely brief mini skirt, low cut blouse, high heeled shoes with no stockings, with a handbag over her shoulder.

The incident called forth a little of the Sherlock Holmes in Gary. He found a fresh used condom near the vehicle. It wasn't yet covered in the ants that were there. As a result it didn't take him long to come to the conclusion that the driver had a woman in the car and there'd been some 'activity' whilst the car was speeding along and crashed. Gary wondered if the missing woman passenger had any part to play in the collision. The wheels had spun so fast the tires were shredded.

He asked the car driver, "Do you know anything about a woman passenger you had with you?"

"No, Sir," he replied but avoided eye contact with Gary.

Gary said, "We'll see."

A short time later the police car arrived back and the officer said,

"We found the girl. She's a prostitute and said she didn't want to get involved. She told us, the man driving the car was a client. Yes, there had been sexual activity while he was driving his vehicle. He did this so that nobody, especially the police, would catch him parked in an alley or parklands with a prostitute."

The result was a collision with the side of the road. The car mounted the nature strip, the wheels spun as the accelerator jammed on. The tyre caught fire and so did the vehicle. The man told the prostitute to run away because he didn't want his wife to see her if she happened to drive past. Gary approached the man with two other officers and told him what the prostitute had told them.

He said, "Yes, that's right. I lied to you because I was petrified my wife and insurance company would find out."

Gary thought, "He still may get badly treated by both."

The man was subsequently charged with Negligent Driving. Gary would have charged him with 'stupidity' had there been such an offence. The woman was a well known prostitute, a highway 'moll' who worked the trucking routes and depots along the Great Western Highway. She could not be charged with anything as she and the driver denied money was exchanged by the act.

Gary reflects how sad it is when people are unfaithful to their spouse. The hurt, pain and drama it causes when the consequences of unfaithfulness come home to roost in their lives. He knows God has the ability to convict of wrongdoings, forgive wrongdoings, reconcile relationships and heal hurts between people who sincerely come to Him in repentance. Repentance means making a 'U' turn away from sin and selfishness to a new life in Christ, through the gospel. People must avoid sin, with God's help, to have peace.

"Too Hot to Handle"

It was one of those days that well and truly proved that Australia is a sun-drenched country. On such a hot day it was even possible to fry an egg on the pavement. Certainly it was the sort of day to make detectives really 'hot under the collar' having to chase criminals. Gary was driving down towards Blacktown Hospital with another detective on this very hot summer day. A call came over the police radio to say there'd been an armed robbery at the hospital. To his surprise, at the same time of the call Gary saw a car speed out of the hospital. Clearly it was the robbers and they recognised Gary and his mate as detectives. They were in an unmarked police car but there was the 'tell tale' two way radio aerial in the middle of the roof with all police vehicles at the time having 3rd month registration labels. They weren't real hard to spot.

Gary forced their car into a gutter and jumped from his police car staying behind the engine bay for cover. Knowing they were armed,

Gary and his partner shouted, with their police revolvers drawn and pointed,

"Get out of the car. Put your hands in the air. Otherwise we'll blow you to kingdom come!"

Gary told me jokingly, "We love that sort of talk."

The suspects were ordered to put hands in the air and not on their heads in case they had guns or knives concealed behind their necks. The aim of yelling was also to intimidate them, for they were dangerous. This was also a psychological ploy to convince them to comply with the police commands. Both robbers got out of their car one on each side. At gunpoint Gary screamed out,

"Put your hands on the roof of the car and spread your legs."

They obeyed but then one of them took his hands off the roof. Gary yelled again,

"Put your hands out on the roof or this will be the most unfortunate day of your life, if you survive it!"

Both men were breathing heavily. At this point Gary and his mate couldn't understand why the two men were very 'jumpy'. Gary said to his mate,

"Watch it mate, I think they're going to do a runner."

Again Gary yelled, "I told you, keep your hands on the roof, and spread your legs."

Both men were making noises, were clearly jittery and the two detectives couldn't work out why. When three or four police cars arrived Gary yelled,

"Check the back seat and boot. Make sure no one else is there. Also check if there are any weapons and clear them."

It was then Gary approached the driver of the car, lifted his hands off the car roof and placed them behind his back in order to handcuff them. As he did so the man breathed out heavily and said,

"Thank God, oh, thank God."

Gary didn't know why he was 'thanking' God so much. It couldn't be that they were caught in the act. It might be they weren't shot by the police? Gary finally asked,

"What are you thanking God for mate?"

He answered, close to tears, "You took my hands off the roof of the car. It's like a barbeque plate. It was scorching hot and I was frightened to take my hands off in case you shot me."

Gary looked at the man's hands which were red raw and blistered. Gary worked out why the men were so 'jumpy'. In the sun, the car's hot roof was more bearable than the pain of being shot by Gary and his mate.

That was the day Gary unintentionally barbequed an armed robber or two! Gary felt sorry for the robbers, but all the police including Gary, laughed at the 'hotplate saga.' Was it police cruelty? Of course it wasn't deliberate. It was just an 'unforeseen' outcome of a good arrest on a hot summer's day.

The robber's guns, disguise and hospital payroll money were recovered. They pleaded guilty and received lengthy gaol terms. Gary explained,

"The robber's hands recovered nicely, after hospital treatment, in the same hospital they held up! I wonder if the doctors and nurses were as gentle with them, as we were. You know what I mean. No doubt their occasional BBQ in gaol, on hot days, will give them 'flashbacks' of the day they were arrested by my mate and me."

"Half a Million for a Dog"

The Police Rescue Squad was called to a house in Dover Heights, a wealthy suburb on the east coast of Sydney. On arrival Gary found general duty police officers were already there having answered a '000' distress call. Gary learned there was an elderly lady whose dog had died. Gary quickly discovered it wasn't just a simple case of a dog dying and the owner grieving. It appeared that when the family discovered how distraught their mother was over the death of the dog, they decided to do something about it. The mother would look out of her window at the things that belonged to her dog. This brought tears to her eyes and upset her even more than she already was. Action was required. The family thought they'd ease their mother's grief and dispose of everything that had belonged to the dog. Out of sight, out of mind was their aim. Unbeknown to the lady, the family threw the dog's kennel, toys, water and food bowls over the cliff at the back of the house. The entire dog's belongings tumbled into the sea far below. They were confident this would relieve their mother and help her grief. With pride they went and told her what they'd done.

When greeted with the news that everything belonging to the dog, including the kennel, had gone over the cliff, the mother shrieked and fainted. She was assisted by her family who were quite upset by her reaction. They sprayed her face with water and called an ambulance. When she sat up she cried hysterically. One of her children asked what was wrong for they believed their mother was still upset over the loss of her dog. Imagine their horror when she finally spoke and said,

"All of my jewels were under the mat in the dog's kennel!"

She screamed out, "I put them in the kennel so that they'd be safe as the dog would guard them!"

The family nearly fainted as well as they reflected on their 'humane act 'gone wrong.

Gary abseiled down the sheer 60m cliff. He searched for any jewels that may not have tumbled into the sea. The water was like a violent washing machine at the edge of the rock platform. After an exhaustive search at the base of the cliff all he could find was an empty and broken ring box. When he gave the mother the empty jewel box and sad news she screamed and fainted again. The jewels were uninsured and a son whispered to Gary they were worth roughly half a million dollars. Treasure lost forever. The moral of the story is, be careful where you store your jewellery. At least tell someone where you keep them and, make sure they are insured. Probably the safest place is in a bank vault, however who wants to keep going to the bank before getting dressed up for a night out? I suppose the dog's kennel is closer? Gary's not sure if the family bought her another dog or more jewellery. Maybe the loss of both again, would be just too much.

CHAPTER EIGHT

A POLITICAL ASSASSINATION

❧

"Assassination is the extreme form of censorship."
George Bernard Shaw, Writer.

"Australia's Political Assassination"

The gentle purr of the police car engine was music to the ears of Acting Inspector Gary Raymond as he guided the machine through the streets of Cabramatta, a Sydney south western suburb. It was a quiet night in Cabramatta for a change, normally not a quiet place to work. There were far too many people who used drugs, guns, knives, stolen goods. The Asian Five 'T' Gang was running rife in those days.

The peace and quiet of Gary's night was suddenly shattered when a call came over the radio,

"A person has been shot. Proceed to Wood Street, Cabramatta."

About 9.30pm, the 5th September 1994. Gary, with many years experience in the force, went to the scene with siren sounding and lights flashing. He had no idea this was no ordinary shooting. When he arrived there were two other police cars at the scene. Gary ran down the driveway. A body was on the ground and two young policemen were carrying out CPR. It didn't take Gary long to realise the victim was John Newman MP, Member of New South Wales State Parliament, the Member for Cabramatta. Gary saw and heard Newman's fiancé Lucy Wang. Wang lived with Newman pending their upcoming wedding. Lucy sat on the doorstep of their house screaming, no shrieking hysterically. She rocked backward and forward as a female police sergeant attempted to comfort her. She kept on yelling,

"He's been shot! He's been shot!"

Her anguish sharply pierced the night air.

Suddenly, Gary was overcome by fear. It dawned on him he didn't know where the offender or offenders were. With his police handgun drawn, his mind raced. Was the gunman in the home, the yard, or the street? Was it a drive by shooting, or did they live next door? As he knelt beside the body, gun scanning the area, he knew his task was to cover the two policemen who were working to save Newman's life by performing CPR. If more bullets were to fly, Gary was ready and waiting to protect them as he waited for back up to arrive. By looking at the shell casings in the driveway it didn't take Gary long to discover Newman, at a guess, had been shot by an automatic handgun of some kind. The bullet had entered through one side of Newman's chest and exited the other side. The two policemen tried desperately to save John, but to no avail. Even as Gary watched, he saw blood and air bubbles oozing from the gunshot wounds, a sure sign of a catastrophic chest intrusion involving the heart and lungs his ambulance experience told him. The ambulance arrived and after an ECG confirmed it was too late to save Newman. Gary knew there was no chance of survival. His life was pronounced extinct by ambulance officers.

John Newman being shot in such horrible circumstances was to shock people across Australia and across the world. Gary knew this would make top headlines in the newspapers. This was only the second Australian political assassination, the first being that of Donald Mackay an anti drug campaigner running for Parliament. Meanwhile the policewoman tried to gain information from Lucy Wang. Although seriously distressed, she gave a brief description of the gunman and the getaway vehicle. More police arrived. Gary gave directions to establish a perimeter, crime scene, protect evidence, tape it off, commence a crime scene log and arrange emergency lighting from police rescue. He directed a search of the immediate area for possible offenders, vehicles, witnesses or other secondary crime scenes. Gary told his team to look for weapons, talk to any witnesses and take note of any cars parked nearby. Even cars driving past were of interest. Every effort was to be made to track the killer or killers early in the investigation. Gary notified senior police and other essential police services to attend the scene. A crowd had gathered so Gary gently moved them back. He later said it was distressing to find that Lucy Wang was still screaming and crying, even though the policewoman tried to comfort her. The crime scene was processed by experts and exhibits collected.

Sometime later, just before the body was to be removed Mrs Naumenko, John Newman's mother and her other son arrived at the scene. They were stressed to the extreme. Gary wasn't sure how they found out about John's death so soon. Media or friends he guessed. They wanted to go to straight to the body but they were restrained by a number of police. Gary said the scene had been cleared of all available evidence. All of the government forensic collection of samples had been done but it was still necessary to keep people away until the government funeral contractors had finished their tasks. Suddenly, so distraught John Newman's mother broke away from the police. She broke through the crime scene tape and ran toward her dead son's body as it lie in the driveway. A number of police officers tried to stop the distressed mother. A frantic struggle took place. Mrs Naumenko screamed and cried hysterically and refused any attempts to halt her progress down the driveway. She broke free but was restrained again. Gary realised how distressing it was for everyone present to see a grieving mother struggle to get to her son's side. Most of all Gary was concerned she might receive a serious injury in the struggle. As a result, police physically escorted her down to her son's body.

When Mrs Naumenko reached the spot, she simply threw herself next to the body restrained by police. She stroked the hair of her dead son. The mother was grief stricken beyond physical measure. As a result of her grief, Gary saw the blood vessels in her nose literally explode! Blood splattered everywhere at high speed over a wide area. Blood from her nose went all over her, even over nearby police, including Gary. Gary quickly put on surgical gloves. He then held Mrs Naumenko's nose to curb the flow of blood. Her tears ran down her chin mixed with her blood, a scene Gary will never forget. Police then stood her to her feet and helped her into the house where her nose was packed by Gary with ice packs taken from the fridge until the arrival of an ambulance. In all of Gary's years as an ambulance officer and police officer, he'd never seen anyone in such anguish and distress that resulted in such a rise of blood pressure causing blood vessels to literally explode in a person's nose like that. To Mrs Naumenko, her son was not a politician but her boy, her little boy. As she wept she told Gary,

"I gave him birth, I fed him from my breasts, I changed his nappy, put him through school, for this?"

Gary comforted her and then prayed with her and John's brother.

John Newman, born John Naumenko on 8th December 1946, the son of Austrian/Yugoslav parents migrated to Australia when he was a child. John Newman was educated at Cabramatta Primary School and Liverpool High School. In March 1972, he changed his name by Deed Poll to Newman so that he would more easily be recognised as an Australian. Newman was elected a member of the New South Wales State Parliament on 1st February 1986 after being chosen in a by election. The assassination was later discussed in the New South Wales Parliament. At this time Mr Hazzard, Member for Wakehurst, said this about John Newman,

"I found John a very determined human being. His perspective on so many issues was born of his background, of his Austrian-Serbian parents and of the circumstances of his young life here. I remember him telling me how hard it was in his young school days when he spoke with an accent. I suppose that was character building."

Hazzard talked about how Newman had suffered a tragic loss when his wife and young child were killed in a car crash. Hazzard said that such things gave Newman a powerful passion for supporting the underdog. Another insight into the mind of John Newman was provided at the same time by another Member of Parliament Mr

Gibson, Member for Londonderry, who said,

"One particular night I asked John about the time he changed his name and the reason for doing so. John said that he saw a goal he thought he had to achieve and this had been the reason for his change of name. I said to him, "How did you settle on a name? It must be terribly hard?" John said he thought it was a new beginning; he was going to be a new person. However, he thought it would be very hard to call himself John 'Newperson'. He said, 'I was a new man." That was his reason for calling himself John Newman. He was a new man. That illustrates the simplicity of the fellow."

During a Four Corners television program in 1997, three years after the assassination, Phuong Ngo, a Cabramatta nightclub owner and political rival of John Newman, said,

"After the murder many media outlets, especially ones run by my opponents in the community, have implied that somehow I was involved in that murder."

As they say, "Where's there's smoke there's fire."

Following the investigation, Phuong Ngo was tried and convicted after many court dramas and locked away for life in a top security gaol. Phuong Ngo was not the one who pulled the trigger or drove the car. The alleged shooter and driver were never convicted due to lack of evidence. The 'code of silence' stopped vital witness testimony. Ngo didn't give evidence against them and the case died down, in spite of heavy media publicity. Maybe one day, Ngo will have a change of heart and conscience and give evidence in court.

It was Sirhan who said of his assassination of Senator Robert Kennedy, "I did it for my country." This certainly could not have been said of Phuong Ngo. On the other hand we can be fairly sure that John Newman would have agreed with Robert Kennedy when he said, "Men are not made for safe havens."

During an ABC Four Corners program, in broken English, Lucy Wang said, "The pain is there always you know. For three years, the pains never go away. Lucy Wang returned to China. To this day, the rest of the murderers who pulled the trigger and the other who drove the car, have not been convicted even though we know who they are, there was no evidence for court. The years have slipped past but the memory lingers on. Cabramatta remains an Asian suburb, mainly Vietnamese. Although there are other nationalities represented the bulk of the population remain Asian. Unfortunately Cabramatta had a long standing heroin problem. John Newman drew attention to the problem and the problem of street gangs dealing in drugs. He was a fearless campaigner. Speaking on television some years after the Newman murder, Sergeant Gordon Connolly of the Cabramatta Police referring to the drug problem in Cabramatta said,

"If you want to call it a war zone, well it's a war and it's your war and my war."

I asked Gary how he felt about this and the Newman affair and he said,

"The thing that crossed my mind, was having seen John Newman previously walking the streets of Cabramatta, standing in Parliament revealing a man full of confidence, a man who was able to subdue any size man with his karate; but then, in that driveway he was lifeless. The very ebb of his life taken out of him by a small piece of lead, called a bullet. It was a real Australian political assassination. He actually sacrificed his life to cause Cabramatta to be librated."

This thought had also run through Gary's mind at the time,

"Who would take his place? Who would be the advocate for Cabramatta after Newman? Who would have the courage that Newman had to bravely stand up to the drug dealers, the drug users, the pimps and the extortionists?"

I asked Gary for further thoughts about the case. He said,

"When Mrs Naumenko broke through the police barrier, I realised that while the police saw John Newman as a murdered politician, Mrs Naumenko saw him as her little boy. The one she had given breath to, probably breast fed, and raised in tough times in a war torn Europe. As I knelt beside her I felt her sheer anguish which was both emotional and physical. I realised the strain had been too much for her body and that's when her nose bled. I also felt sorry for Lucy Wang. One minute she had everything and the next thing her whole life was turned around. She had nothing. She really loved her John."

One thing is sure; Cabramatta has never been the same since the shooting of John Newman. The government of the day was grossly neglectful of Cabramatta until John's murder, then funding came pouring in allowing Police operations to clean up Cabramatta. The police and community had a gutful of crime and little resources. Gary and his mates hit the gangs hard and fast with amazing success. The gangs were decimated by good police work and the courts. They no longer exist and it's now a safe place to live and visit. Tim Priest has written about Cabramatta and is strong advocate for effective law enforcement.

"Police are very effective in what we do, if we're given the people, money and time, to do what we know best.......lock up crooks", Gary said passionately.

"The Asian restaurants, fabric shops and produce markets are fantastic and shouldn't be missed", Gary said licking his lips.

Gary wrapped up the event for me when he recalled a scripture found in the book of Ecclesiastes, *"No man knows when his time will come. As fish caught in a cruel net, or birds are taken in a snare, so men are trapped by evil times that fall unexpectedly upon them."* *(Ecclesiastes 9:12 NIV)*

Gary told me, "As an ambo and cop, I saw that people can be taken from time into eternity in a second. For us the fact of life at Cabramatta was that the law enforcement arm of government was grossly under resourced."

Gary had high hopes that the government might listen to the needs highlighted by this incident. He sadly realises governments are far too slow to act. They respond politically for votes rather than the needs on the ground. Hopefully, it would have been a good adage if observed, 'It's an ill wind that blows nobody any good'. Of one thing we can be sure, nobody is safe from a speeding bullet. Not even a local politician.

He said, "After the murder, the government gave Cabramatta the needed funding to successfully clean up the streets, which we did. Police operations plus Fairfield Council CCTV gave us good tools." An attempt to prove Phuong Ngo's innocence came to a Sydney

Court in 2009, but his appeal was quashed. He remains in Australia's top security jail at Goulburn in the southern highlands of New South Wales at this time. It has been said, "For want of a nail, the shoe is lost, for want of a shoe, the horse is lost, and for want of a horse, the ruler is lost." So it was with John the 'new man'.

- CHAPTER NINE -

THE SHIELD OF FAITH

"The righteous will live by his faith."
Habakkuk 2:4 (600BC Jewish Prophet)

"A Bold Testimony"

Gary told me an incredible story of his life. I sat and listened with awe. Gary commenced,

"When I started school, I remember helping kids who fell in the playground or standing close by staring at a teacher who was rendering first aid to an injured child, waiting to help if required. When I was about five years old in class, there was an almighty loud screech of tyres and a crash at the corner of my school, the New Lambton Primary School near Newcastle. I sensed people must be hurt because of the loud bang and crunching sound. I wanted to go out and have a look because I couldn't see it from my window. I stood up. The teacher said, "Sit down Gary" and she went outside to look. I followed her and was sternly told to go back to my desk. I remember to this day, I couldn't rest not knowing whether the injured people were getting quick help although, I just wanted to look and see what the policemen and ambulance men were going to do. These were flashbacks to when I was on the bus as a young boy with mum. I carried this inner drive right into adulthood.

As David previously told you, we had a notorious intersection at Hobart Road and Wallarah Road, New Lambton, just down the road from our house at 23 Thalaba Road. We'd hear the screech of brakes, a deep loud crunch and scraping on the road followed by deathly silence. Sometimes a neighbour would knock on the door loudly and ask if I was home because there was an accident on the corner with people injured. In either case, I'd grab my first aid kit. Mum would grab a couple of blankets and we'd run to the corner to render assistance. As I wasn't able to pursue my passion becoming a doctor, I became disinterested in school, did poorly in exams and became interested in playing outdoors in rain, hail or shine. I loved going out playing with my brothers and mates in the backyard, bush, in swamps, storm water drains, disused mine shafts the beach and even under our house. I relished adventure.

I earned money on a paper run in Newcastle city and bought a pushbike. I calculated the newsagent was ripping off my tips. He denied it and called me a liar. I left the job and left the afternoon papers on a bus seat for people to take free as a payback.

During this time I attended the New Lambton and then Lambton Salvation Army Sunday Schools. I learnt the facts from the Bible that God created everything, that Jesus Christ was born from a virgin, lived a sinless life as God the Son, died by crucifixion to take the punishment for my sin on His shoulders, rose from the dead and is coming back to make things right again soon.

I had no trouble believing these facts, and at a young age, remember telling my father and mother I'd received Jesus as my Saviour and had asked Him to forgive my sin. In Sunday school I played up, because having four brothers and then being suddenly thrust into a room full of girls, I began attention seeking behaviour. Rightfully, this got me thrown out and told to sit on the front step of the church. I received attention alright. At the end of the class, Doreen (Topsy) Buttery, the Young People's Sergeant Major (Sunday school teacher), called me back in and gave me a one to one lesson. Looking back, I'm so grateful she did what I now consider as 'gospel intensive care'. I can't wait to see her in heaven and thank her for that commitment and care of a naughty boy. She said once, "Gary God came in Jesus to 'rescue' you from the penalty of your sin. Using the word rescue, little did she know that one day I'd be a member of the elite Police Rescue Squad.

I began to go to Boys Legion and Cliff Davis taught me to play the cornet. Cliff was a brilliant euphonium player and dedicated many hours to me and other kids getting to the stage of playing in the Salvation Army Band. I went to open air meetings and played in the band. Hot nights, cold nights, wet nights it didn't matter, we were there on the streets playing music and giving out the gospel message. We used kerosene lanterns at night to see the music. Often we marched to and from the open air meetings. One night after Bandmaster Len Randall dropped me off at home in his FJ Holden he paused and said, "Gary, you need to know that God has an amazing plan for your life." It didn't mean much to be then, but sure does now. I can't wait to see Len and the others in heaven who have influenced my life for Jesus.

During his time I became a member of the Royal Australian Navy Sea Cadet Reserve at the Training Ship Tobruk, Nobby's Beach. We wore the real naval uniform, did parade ground drill and marching, learnt seamanship on Newcastle Harbour in a 27 ft former whaler. We travelled to Sydney on some weekends to stay on board real war ships like the HMAS Anzac, HMAS Vendetta and many more. I contemplated a career in the Navy. However, the thought of signing up for nine years didn't attract me, especially if I got sea sick!

Regrettably, under the influence of my Navy cadet mates and a need to be accepted, admired and part of the crowd, I began for the first time drinking and smoking. I was about thirteen years old. My mother smelt my breath one day. She bought a packet of smokes and told me to go into the bathroom and smoke the whole packet one cigarette after the other in an effort to put me off smoking. It worked the opposite. I loved smoking and pretended I wanted to vomit just to satisfy her need to rehabilitate me. At this point I lived a double life. I was a Salvo one day and drunken sailor the next. It didn't worry me doing it, just getting caught was uncomfortable. I stupidly followed the crowd. I was too scared, or too stupid to say, "No."

At sixteen years old, I left home for Sydney as I'd won a cadetship with the New South Wales Ambulance Service. My mother, through the Salvos, found a boarding house in Marrickville managed by a Salvo lady named May Jensen. I shared a room there with another bloke and was well looked after by May. I became attracted to her daughter, Jennifer, and we became friends. Over the years this grew to love and we began to date. My ambulance training went for two years at Ambulance HQ and Royal Prince Alfred Hospital and was fascinating. Every spare moment I spent at the hospital mortuary watching autopsies. I remember being amazed at human anatomy and physiology. I loved studying it. We trained in the emergency department, medical, obstetrical, surgical wards and completed the nurse's initial training course. One day I got in trouble with the tutor, Sister Fisher for putting a lighted cigarette into the training skeleton's mouth. However, I came first in one of my final courses at the Ambulance Training School. On my time off, I again began to drink, smoke and party hard with my other cadet mates and again, lived a double life while attending the Marrickville Salvation Army church to please my parents. I moved out of May's boarding house to Petersham and later shared a small flat in Enmore with Paul Hancock, another ambulance cadet.

At the age of eighteen I graduated as a fully qualified ambulance officer stationed at Quay Street HQ in the centre of Sydney. We covered the Sydney CBD, Redfern, Kings Cross and much more. I was called out to many situations such as shootings, stabbings, attempt suicides, road trauma, industrial accidents, assaults, baby deliveries, cardiac arrests, strokes, overdoses and rescues. I coped well and loved every minute of it. I was always pleased to be called out to a casualty critical incident. Being in the thick of tragedy was satisfying for me. My early indoctrination into first aid with St. John was invaluable.

During my ambulance work, I completed rescues alongside the famous New South Wales Police Rescue Squad. The late Sergeant Ray Tyson, Officer in Charge, Police Rescue told me after a job that I had a very good ability to stay calm in crisis situations and I should consider resigning from the ambos and joining the police to get into his squad. This was confirmed by the late Sergeant Bill Fahey in a subsequent conversation at a cliff rescue scene.

After three years on the road as an ambo, and with the prestige of being in the Police Rescue Squad, I decided to leave the ambos and join the police. On graduation from the Police Academy, I was stationed at Redfern, Mascot and Botany on general duties for about a year and in 1973, was accepted as the seventh member of elite police rescue squad. That was the biggest thrill of my life. I felt so proud in those white overalls and being with a great group of men.

There was no rescue school, you learnt on the job in those days. I was 'thrown in the deep end' straight away. I learnt fast under the 'fatherly' supervision of wonderful sergeants including the late Sergeant Joe Beecroft. The late Sergeant Ray Tyson said, "Boy, there is no-one to rescue the rescuer. There is no police rescue, to rescue the police rescue." What he meant was that if I got trapped on a mission, there was nobody to rescue me, the rescuer. Failure on a rescue mission was not in his mindset nor should be in mine. The late Sergeant Bill Fahey told me not to get emotionally involved. He told me not to cry about a rescue as it would damage me emotionally, undermine police rescue's reputation as tough blokes and our ability to cope as a team. He said, "Gaz, if we lose it, everyone else will."

He was right. I understand what he was saying. We held everyone together by our example. Many relied on us in the worst circumstances. The late Sergeant Joe Beecroft told me that if I wanted to leave Police Rescue at any time I could, as the normal police tenure of three years didn't apply at rescue. He also made it clear that the boss could tell me to go without notice if he thought I wasn't coping. I understood what they were saying. Stay strong and never let it get to you as that was dangerous on the job. We had to stay focused. To be distracted could be fatal. Such an approach, put pressure on the squad to perform at our best all the time, in all situations. I can understand the tough approach as to fail might have meant death or serious injury to rescuer or victim. They were all proud to say that the Police Rescue Squad never lost a member in the workplace or injured anyone on a mission during their existence from 1942 to the present time. In the squad, my medical skills were invaluable as many patients were inaccessible and needed pre hospital care before we moved them. I also began teaching first aid to other squad members and squad recruits. I designed and manufactured marine plywood spinal fracture lifting boards that could be used at both the foot and head ends. The American boards had a foot and head end which was confusing, especially in the dark. I updated the medical equipment carried by the squad.

Exposed to dangerous situations made us a very close knit group of men. We relied on each other to stay alive. As well as rescue operatives, we were all police officers. That brought extra danger and pressure as we were heavily involved in bomb disposal, armed offender situations, suicide negotiations, searches for criminals or evidence, public riots or protestors occupying structures. We required the skill of arresting people, collecting evidence and give testimony in court, which we did. Our reputation as being skilled, courageous and hard men made me independent. I was a very confident person happy in my own skin. I became totally insular and detached from tragedy or its consequences.

Death didn't cause me to grieve for anyone, as I had no control over death anyway. I recovered dead bodies of all ages in all conditions, whether decomposed, maggot ridden, eaten by animals, cut into pieces, ripped apart, squashed, beheaded, burnt or buried. I handled them all without flinching. I was there in my rescue squad overalls and nobody else was going to do the dirty jobs, except us.

My pride after getting awards and commendations for my rescue work puffed me up and made me feel elitist and superior to others. The squad relished the media attention, and so should we. We did things not many were game enough to do. People would shout me beers in the pub all night if they saw me on the television news doing what they perceived as a 'heroic' act. For me, it was just another rescue job. All these inner emotional conflicts later caused some serious personal issues. I was getting too self sufficient and stoic. It was not the way I was brought up or what I learnt in Sunday school or church.

I'd given up going to the Salvation Army church years before. I was outwardly friendly, but had a heart of stone. A friend told me my heart had become harder than a brick. I didn't see it. Like some other elitist units in the police and defence forces, we developed a 'work hard play hard' culture. We drank hard, ate hard and partied hard. This, plus being on twenty four hour call, made it hard on our families and friends. A number of those relationships didn't survive the test of time and pressure. God was ignored. I didn't need Him as I was self sufficient. Besides, He might put a stop to my self gratification. In other words, 'spoil my fun'.

Jenny and I finally decided, against our parent's wishes, to live together as a defacto couple. We were later married. Our marriage was like any other except the pressure of the police culture, shift work and an on call status gave us restricted time together. The fact we'd both stopped going to church at the Salvation Army, began drinking and smoking, started a downward spiral in our marriage. Long hours away from home rescuing and when I could and should have been at home, I was out partying with the boys from the squad took its toll. Jenny was doing shift work at Canterbury Public Hospital Emergency Department, which added to restricted time together. We had an amicable and friendly relationship, but grew apart with nothing much in common.

Again, off duty I began to fall into the drinking, smoking and party lifestyle. I wasn't stressed by work, just loved having what I perceived a good time with lots of self indulgence. I used imaginary stress at work for an excuse to party however, that was just a cover for bad behaviour. It was as if I was saying to the world, "I picked up bits of a human being and put them into a body bag under a train today. So world, I am going to party hard tonight and feel good." It was almost like a reward for putting me on the frontline and doing the dirty work. Because of my 'self centred' attitude my communication with mum and dad (visits, letters or phone calls) waned. Mum subtly reminded me to keep in touch as they loved news of my life. I loved rescue work and couldn't wait to get a call out as it was an opportunity to practise my medical/ rescue skills and show off to those around me. I had very high self esteem and felt invincible and valuable to the world.

One weekend late in November 1979, Jenny said she was going to the south coast with some girlfriends to look at art galleries. On the Sunday night of that weekend I drove to a local petrol station near our home. Unexpectedly, I saw Jenny with a man swapping clothes from his vehicle to hers in the car park. Confused and shocked I asked what she was doing and why. I wondered where the girls she allegedly went away with for the weekend were. She said she would explain later. Back at home she said she was leaving me and moving in to live with that man in the car across the road, an ambulance officer named Trevor. Jenny hurriedly went into the bedroom to pack some belongings and left with Trevor. I asked her to stay and talk it through with me. She refused. I needed at least some answers.

When she left I was scared, alone. I wasn't angry just emotionally numb and dazed. I couldn't stop shaking. This was so unexpected. Looking back, I should have been more aware of our failing relationship. Self centeredness has its own consequences. I had no idea she was having an affair and she didn't know what I was doing either. I suffered badly during the next few weeks. I wasn't game enough to tell anyone. I was saving face I suppose, or maybe I thought she may come back and give us another go at the marriage. I had no sleep. It was torture. I tried to contact her without success. How would I live without her? Was she really a 'life support system?' Was this the end of my life as I knew it?

During this depressing time I was expected to perform highly dangerous rescues that took all of my concentration mentally and emotionally whilst thinking about my recently failed marriage. I was preoccupied and had to pull myself into gear, keeping focused on the rescue job at hand. Only a lapse for a moment might have cost someone's life. Rescue requires a high level of physical, mental and emotional performance. I could little afford even a second of 'mind off the job.' Even when negotiating with suicidal people, I thought, "It is me who should be jumping, not you."

I made discreet enquires about Trevor and found out he worked at Campsie Ambulance Station and had left his wife, Heidi for Jenny. I later spoke to Heidi, a lovely person and she too was broken hearted and confused. We shared our grief but there was no solution. Both lost in an 'empty space'. Driven by the need for answers, I went to the ambulance station and confronted Trevor. He was scared but stayed calm. He couldn't look me in the eye. I asked him straight out whether he loved Jenny. He said he loved her. I left without further conversation. I heard later he was terrified and thought I was going to shoot him. I then recalled I was on duty and armed when I spoke to him. The thought of shooting him never actually occurred to me, so looking back it's quite amusing. I found out they were living in St Peters. I drove past during the day and night hoping to catch a glimpse of Jenny and engage in conversation. The 'why question' haunted me. Was there a chance of talking her into coming back home? I looked for answers and some indication as to our future. I wasn't sleeping and when I did had nightmares. I wasn't eating either and wasn't game to drink alcohol. I had enough trouble coping without being drunk.

Late at night on 29th November 1979, I was home alone and sober for a change. I was in a depressed state and reflective mood looking over my life up to now. I walked around our house in St John's Park looking at things that, prior to the previous Sunday I'd shared with Jenny with whom I had intended to spend the rest of my life. She'd left all of these memories to eat away at me as well. She was my first love, or so I thought. Reflecting, was it love or just the idea of love? I wandered round the house. I looked at photos as well as clothes left behind in wardrobes. It was hard. My own behaviour and abandonment of God weighed heavily on my heart. I saw my errors. They teach you in policing to look for hazards and calculate countermeasures, but this break up came suddenly. I was not prepared. I tried to keep a brave face but inside was torn apart, falling to pieces. As Joni Erickson sings, 'I'm sunny on the outside, but raining on the inside'. I realised being alone and lonely were two separate circumstances. I couldn't see a future for myself and being alone, and loneliness was the pits.

I started strolling from room to room. I wanted to cry but there was pressure in the rescue squad not to cry or lose your self control. It was seen as a sign of weakness to not cope and seen as a risk to the reputation of the squad. Everyone else can fall apart but not police rescue men. We were not only performing rescues, but being police officers as well. We were the toughest, and the last standing. I remembered again what one of my sergeants had told me, "There's no one to rescue the rescue squad." He was right. There was no room to fail on rescue missions. I'd been successful in all of my rescue missions; however my life's mission was failing badly.

Entering any room which had a mirror on the wall I would stop, stare at myself, and talk myself into calming down and keeping control. I was gritting my teeth, pointing at myself saying, "Pull yourself together, don't lose it, keep tough, you can do it. Remember who you are." When I finished the self talk I felt worse, knowing I didn't even have the ability to talk myself down, let alone other depressed people. I was reaching the bottom of the barrel. My survival skills as a man, a cop and a husband were fast running on empty. Questions with no answers ran through my mind. Did she leave because I was not a good friend and provider? Was I too busy with work, too much of a party boy with my mates, no common interests, not a good communicator?

The rejection I felt was too much. I wanted to escape this sad and hopeless world. I felt useless and a failure. The emotional pain was too much to bear. As my mind wandered from one thing to another, I thought of all the death, suffering, grief, sights, smells, sounds, deathly silences, and physical touches of rescue. Yet I'd never cried, nor worried in the past. I guess I was more sensitive to grief during this time of my own personal loss. A bit of a 'pity party' I guess.

At the depth of my hopelessness and hurt that night, I remembered that in a drawer in my bedroom was my loaded police issue Smith & Wesson .38 revolver with six bullets in the cylinder. We kept our gun at home on call in those days. I didn't want to die, but the emptiness and emotional pain I felt was seemingly beyond repair. I saw no future. I didn't touch the gun but just stared at it lying there begging to be used to end my misery. I was so shocked that I, the confident and in control Gary Raymond, police rescue man had even thought of suicide.

I realised I'd talked dozens back from jumping off The Gap, buildings, bridges or towers and I now needed to negotiate with myself for my own life. It was a shock. It was nothing I could have predicted. My headache thumped, my throat was dry and my stomach was in knots. I was shaking and weak at the knees, sucked dry, sapped of life itself. Suffering self pity I wanted to cry, but couldn't for it wasn't allowed. I was a tough rescue man, remember?

As I searched my mind and the depths of my heart, my Sunday school days returned to my thoughts. I remember my teacher had said, "Gary, God came in Jesus to rescue you from the penalty of your sin". A light switched on in my soul. That was it. The rescuer needed rescuing. I remembered Jesus died to take my sin on Himself, to save me from God's punishment for my sins. Jesus took my blame, my failures and my rebellion at His death. He rose from the dead to show He was God and was able to save me from a messy life here on earth and an eternity in hell. All God wants is to have me with Him in this life, and later in heaven for my eternity.

In fact there is a rescuer to rescue the rescuer, and His name is Jesus. He is the only Mediator between God and mankind.

I walked away from the gun.

I took a big breath in and burst into tears crying uncontrollably. I fell to the floor of the lounge room on my elbows and knees yelling out, "Jesus I need you now!" I was spiritually heavy with my sin, I needed to know forgiveness and surrender to God. Even though I was a supposedly a 'rescue hero' I still had offended God and rebelled against Him.

All of my good works and brave rescues could not save me, only Jesus could save me. As I pleaded those words, I waited on the Lord. I surrendered to His love; grace and mercy as He poured His precious blood out to wash me clean. His presence came into my heart and soul by His Holy Spirit. I was filled with God. I felt a peace and relief like a burden had been lifted off me. I kept crying and thanked God for responding to my rescue call. I decided to hand my life and future over to Him. I asked God to give me the faith and trust in His plan for my life with or without Jenny.

I also asked Him to heal me from the past effects of my rescue work specially, my hard heart. I asked God to take away all of my independence, and help me to be dependent on Him.

On that lounge room floor, I gained a new assurance God was healing me of the hurts of my marriage breakdown and would be with me during this troubled time. I prayed He'd give me the ability to forgive Jenny and Trevor as well.

I stood up and rang my brother Neil and his wife Marilyn with all the details. Neil rang the Salvation Army's Major Hilton Harmer who came to my house late that night. He explained the gospel, along with the biblical requirements of the decision that I had made for Christ, and prayed with me.

I gave up drinking alcohol that night however; smoking took a little bit longer. That night I rang my parents. They were disappointed with the marriage break up. Mum was pleased, but not surprised, I had come back to Christ. She'd prayed for me every day since I showed I could live without God. Jenny's mother, May Jensen, told me she was very sad her daughter had gone off with another man. She assured me I would 'find someone else someday'. She was pleased I'd made things right with God and looked forward to the day when Jenny would do the same. She told me that Jenny's boyfriend Trevor was from New Zealand and he had a Christian background, as well as his family.

I thought to myself, "The best way to muck up your life and your eternity is to push God aside." I had proven it until my decision to come back to His love and plan. I told Jenny that I had committed my life back to Christ. It made her even more determined to divorce me. God was not in her life's plan at that time and she finally did divorce me and married Trevor. Sadly, after having two daughters, Trevor left Jenny for another woman. One of Jenny's daughters has proudly joined the Queensland Police Force.

The following Sunday morning after I had been on the floor, I went to the Salvation Army Congress Hall church in Sydney where

Neil and Marilyn were heavily involved. I made a public decision for Christ. I then attended the Salvos at Fairfield, making it my regular church close to home. Over the ensuing months I grew in the knowledge of God through my Bible and started to tell others about Him and what He'd done for me. I learnt to pray and had a peace in my heart I'd never had before. I was forgiven and a new creation."

I told a Christian police officer that I'd given my life to Christ. He looked at me suspiciously and said, "Alright Gaz, what's the punch line?" He thought I was having a go at him. I said with a tear in my eye, "No mate it's true." He looked stunned. "You?" he asked. I said, "Yes mate, me." He said, "Wow, I don't believe it. I apologise sincerely Gaz I never prayed for you. I thought you were too tough for God." The officer and I shared many things in our faith journey that day. I thought later, "What a letdown. The first Christian cop you tell you have become one of them, didn't believe me. It reminds me now of the Apostle Paul. After his conversion, people were in disbelief at first and were scared of him. It makes me laugh now."

I was stunned at Gary's story thus far. It proved that what we muck up, God fixes up.

Gary continued.

"Sometime later, I noticed a beautiful brown eyed, brown haired primary school teacher named Michelle at my Salvo's church. She was very pretty, had a big heart, a lady like outlook and a great personality. We became friends and shared many aspects of our personal lives, including my police rescue commitment. One evening I plucked up the courage to tell her I was in love with her and she said she loved me very much too. I was thrilled to bits at such deep love that I had never felt before for anybody. It wasn't just my love this time, but Christ's love flowing through me to her and vice versa. It was new and different. That started a deep spiritual and loving relationship. We were married on 9th January, 1982 at the Salvation Army, Parramatta.

Early in our marriage Michelle displayed a wonderful ability to cope with my police work, especially my call outs late at night and early hours of the morning. I'd often arrive home physically tired after a rescue, wearing blood soaked overalls. I'd shower, soak my overalls and without fuss, Michelle washed and ironed them. In later years we were able to get our rescue overalls done in a commercial laundry through work. She was patient and understanding when we were attending weddings, church or social events and when a rescue call came in.

Michelle was often left alone at the event and made her own way home. She never complained openly, but I'm sure it wasn't easy. Her strong relationship with God and her faith and trust in Him to look after me during rescue or hostile policing missions sustained her. She's a good listener, a sensible advisor, very practical and I attribute my emotional stability today to her deep level of love and care for me. Michelle would listen to me relate my feelings after I returned home from a horrible rescue, although there were many other experiences that best stayed at work or in the dark corners of my mind, for obvious reasons.

I have never met a person like Michelle for helping people who have all manner of needs. She is a spontaneous responder with determination to help. As a caring teacher, she is loved and admired by everyone for her teaching and organising abilities. Nothing is too much trouble for her. She is firm, but fair with the kids, bringing out the best in them. She is clever at art, handicrafts, and games. She can read children like they are an 'open book'. She has probably taught about a thousand or more children over her career thus far, a God given achievement. She goes to events out of school hours, which her children are performing in, to support their efforts. Michelle is rich in wisdom. Often we'll be with people chatting away. Michelle doesn't say much but when she does, everyone stops to listen. We love animals especially our Miniature Schnauzer, Oskar. His antics give us so many laughs and what a faithful 'mate' he is. I still love Michelle as much now, as the first day we met. I am so grateful to God for this gift of a loving and faithful wife with whom I can share everything."

As Gary related his experiences, I thought how his life was like a diamond, multifaceted. Gary continued,

"Michelle is an only child as her mother nearly died during her pregnancy with Michelle. She was strongly advised by doctors not to have any more children. Michelle's dad collapsed and died of a heart attack on Father's Day some years ago. He was a stock car racing driver early in his life (Australasian Champion) and sold big trucks for a living. I know where Michelle acquires her love of cars and anything 'automobile'. I didn't get to meet Michelle's dad, but heard good things about him as a husband to Betty and dad to Michelle. Michelle often tells me that her dad would have loved me and we would have enjoyed each other's company. It's a pity I didn't get to meet him. Michelle as a teenager asked her dad could she buy a Mini. He said, "No." Years later, she asked me and I said, "Yes of course Darling." Michelle's mum and extended family, the Lees, are good to us and I love them each. We have great times with them.

As a new Christian, I continued to read my Bible and pray. I investigated evolution and found it to be a hoax. The evidence is clear, as the Bible tells us, in the beginning God created the heavens and the earth, along with all living things. Science shows more than enough evidence of a Creator God in all His design. I was excited to find out that Jesus died, was resurrected and is coming back to rescue me, if I don't see Him first, in my death. The Bible tells us death is not the end; it's you personally, separating from your earthly body, to go into your eternal life. We even receive a brand new body suited to living in eternity. No pain, bloodshed or suffering ever again so the Bible says. How good is that?

I grew in spiritual maturity to the point of being comfortable telling others about Jesus love and His forgiveness, through repentance. I began keynote speaking to church and community groups and saw God in action as He called people to follow Him. I met other Christian police, ambulance officers, fire fighters, rural fire, VRA and SES members. Our fellowship at the Christian Police Fellowship of NSW meetings was enormous encouragement and help. I gained a loving drive to help cops to respond to Jesus.

I also witnessed to God's love both on and off duty to victims of crime, witnesses of crime, and yes offenders that I had arrested.

I could never see any difference between my police work and my Salvation Army work. It was only different uniforms. I began doing Christian street teamwork in the Blacktown area on a Drug Arm van, and helped many abandoned young people. They knew I was an off duty cop but instead of that repelling them, it attracted them as I helped those though difficult times in their lives. I was able to pray with them and organise practical help. I often acted as sort of liaison between the street gangs and the cops. Being at street level, I was given lots of information with some turning out to be good intelligence on crime around the area and beyond. I passed that information to our Intelligence Officer at work, resulting in successful crime solving. Encouraging people who were reported as missing to contact police or home was another advantage of being on the streets, off duty. God protected us as we broke up fights, rescued girls from sexual assaults, prevented suicides, helped robbery victims, and rendered first aid for stabbings, pedestrian collisions and overdoses before police and ambulance officers arrived. It gave me a different perspective to being on duty in a police car. I learnt just as much off duty as on duty.

I worked as a volunteer chaplain to the Salvation Army Emergency Services (SAES) with Major Frank Wilson. We lectured on Critical Incident Stress Awareness and prepared Salvationists in New South Wales and Queensland to help themselves and others in disaster events. We also came across many people who needed prayer and a good listening ear as they recalled their own past traumatic incidents.

On police patrol in Cabramatta and later Blacktown, God showed me how I could approach gang members, drug dealers, drug users and prostitutes, and tell them Jesus loved them and wanted to forgive them allowing them to be born again into a new life. This did not disrupt my police work. If required, I would arrest them for offences and still maintain my Christian witness. Often after the 'official' police interview was over, I'd engage in conversation and plead with them to accept Christ.

I'd often engage with their family, whether they were functional or not. I was often called by other police to pacify disturbed people

THE SHIELD OF FAITH

in custody or help them with seeking accommodation, food, clothing or rehabilitation for their prisoners prior to release on bail. This also gave me an opportunity to discuss God's love with all concerned.

As a Christian police officer, I became acutely aware of the danger people were in if they heard the gospel news and still rejected God. The thought of anyone spending an eternity in hell was horrible to me. Just as I rescued people as a rescue squad officer, God rescued me. I felt a strong need to tell people, if they wanted to listen, how Christ took our sin on Himself, could rescue them and bring them to Heaven for eternity.

Today, as I allow God the Holy Spirit to have His way in me, I continue to speak to people on a one to one basis about God, whenever the opportunity arises. My 'warning ministry' to people, that Jesus is coming back again soon, is strong. As a cop, I warned many people of impending danger – floods, fires, hazardous materials or armed offenders. I feel I must continue to warn people who reject Christ, to tell them about His salvation. The thought of their eternity in hell terrifies me.

I really enjoy my friends that I work with now in Rotary International Blacktown City. I am chaplain to the Police Post Trauma Support Groups NSW and I'm a member of the Christian Police Fellowship NSW. I am on the State Committee of Management Retired Police Association NSW and the Welfare Officer of the Retired Police Association Parramatta/the Hills Branch. I work with Ian Powell who is the Organisational Risk Manager Salvation Army and attend Salvation Army Parramatta Corps when possible. I also work with Paul Shrubb of Risk, Response and Rescue and I'm involved in several other organisations. My life is fulfilled contributing to these dedicated people and them to me. I have learnt a so much from them which has enriched my life."

CHAPTER TEN

RISKS GALORE

"When men are pure, laws are useless, when men are corrupt,
laws are broken."
Benjamin Disraeli, British Prime Minister.

"Gun at Chest"

Gary and his partner, the late Detective Sergeant Bob Broad, were in
old jeans doing plain clothes surveillance work. They were unshaven
and untidy to blend in 'with the crowd'. They were following drug
dealers and break and enter offenders in cars borrowed by the police
from second hand car dealers, again to blend in. Their guns were
hidden in ankle holsters under their trouser leg and the police radio
was hidden at the back of the glove box.

Maria, the 'madam' in a brothel had witnessed a prostitute being
killed by two standover men in Kings Cross. These men found
out the madam may have witnessed the murder hiding behind her
reception desk and set out to find her. To them she was a witness and
had to be eliminated. A prostitute rang the lady and told her the men
were coming to her house after her. After a struggle in her mind, she
finally rang the police.

As a result, an urgent call came through on the police radio for
any police to attend and protect the woman whilst waiting for the
State Protection Group to come from the city. Gary heard the call
on his portable radio and told his mate the woman's house was just
around the corner from them. They replied to the call and attended.
When they arrived at the house they knocked on the front door and

said, "Open up, it's the police; we're here to protect you."

The woman opened the front door, then screen door and to Gary's utter surprise, she lunged forward jabbing a loaded rifle barrel into Gary's chest. Shocked, he looked down in disbelief. She had her finger on the trigger. It looked like it was loaded with an ammunition clip and was cocked. Gary instinctively put his hands up in the air as a 'surrender gesture'.

Gary said, "What are you doing? Stop this. We're police, here to help. Put the gun down now."

The two detectives tried to explain they were police but the woman screamed that she didn't believe them. Gary tried to reassure the woman, but the trouble was he and his partner certainly didn't look like police being unshaven in their old untidy clothes. Gary couldn't reach for his gun to protect himself as it was in his ankle holster. He really thought the woman was going to shoot. He kept begging her not to. She had glazed eyes staring at Gary. She cried, shook and growled with white foamy spittle between her lips like stalagmites or stalactites,

"You're not going to kill me, like you killed her."

Gary fearfully realised the woman thought he and his partner were gang members from Kings Cross coming to kill her! Gary tried to slowly move back, she pushed forward still pressing the gun hard into his chest yelling she would kill them. Gary thought of knocking the gun to his side with his forearm however, with her finger on the trigger, the gun could have fired accidentally, let alone deliberately. His partner wasn't game to bump the gun either for the same reason. Bob was frozen knowing any action could kill Gary and himself. Gary pleaded,

"We're police in plain clothes. Don't shoot, please don't shoot. We are not the blokes from the Cross"!

She continued to scream and cry with utter fear in her eyes.

Talking to Gary about this incident he said,

"The Bible tells us that death is a high risk factor in the world we're in. It's a dangerous place. It says we're all waiting to die one way or another. We live our lives to the full, but in the police force we must always be ready to die. That's not being melodramatic, it's a reality. It's extremely rare to die on duty, but it's possible".

Gary and his partner kept their hands up in surrender to her. Gary's thoughts raced. His heart was thumping nearly out of his chest. He couldn't think of a way to get out of his situation alive. He thought of his impending death. He would not have a chance to say goodbye to Michelle, although he'd given her a cuddle and kiss when he left for work. "Die now? God is this your time for me?" he thought. Gary had things to do, things to achieve, things to finish, people to help, places to go. It looked desperate as Gary slowly and forcefully said,

"Madam, we're police officers. Please put the gun down and let us help you".

She didn't comprehend or respond. Her mind was locked up. She was shaking uncontrollably. Gary thought,

"If I grab the gun and get shot at least my partner will disarm her and live". But then he thought, "What if she shoots him too?"

It's better to stay still. Don't even breathe. Nothing was working. Like a hold on his life. Gary thought it's not if he would be shot, it's when he would be shot.

Gary knew he was right with God as he had given his life to Jesus through repentance. He remembered the Bible says, 'to be absent from the body, is to be present with the Lord'. Gary knew that he would be with Jesus quickly as his body would be dead on the porch. Gary prayed silently, gripped his teeth together and held his breath waiting for a bullet to thunder through his chest. He even wondered what it was going to be like to be shot and die. Would it be quick, slow, numb or painful? He had run out of options to save his life. He was still in denial and disbelief that he was in this life threatening position when he'd come to help and protect someone! Time seemed to have stopped. Gary was in a mental vacuum, like a tunnel with just the three of them. Gary gave up and waited. His partner did the same. Both were mentally exhausted. At that moment, probably supernaturally induced by God, Gary looked over the woman's shoulder. Hanging on the back wall of her hallway he saw a crucifixion symbol, a wooden cross with silver metallic Jesus on it.

A real peace came over Gary; a peace that the Bible says "passes all understanding, not the peace the world gives".

Gary quietly and exhausted said,

"Look Maria, I'm a committed Christian Police Officer. I love Jesus and I care about you. If you shoot me, the Bible says I'll be going straight to be with Jesus in heaven. I forgive you and so will He".

Maria stared at Gary eye to eye. He stared back for what seemed an eternity but was only seconds. Gary grinned at her in a comforting way. Without warning, she withdrew the gun from pressing into his chest, lowered it, and handed the gun to Gary. He handed it to his partner who cleared it and rendered it safe. Gary saw a bullet drop out of the breach onto the porch. A cold chill went down his spine with the thought that it may have ended up through his heart.

It took a few seconds but Gary now realised his life was preserved. He clicked back into 'tactical mode' and took the woman into the centre of the house as he was now afraid the men may drive by. Gary gently arrested Maria who cried uncontrollably. Gary immediately realised, Maria was going to shoot him in the 'front' and the gangsters might drive by and shoot him in the 'back'. Guns drawn, covering the front and back doors, waiting for assistance, they were all lying on the kitchen floor. The woman was still weeping and apologised to both detectives. Gary allowed her to wipe her nose with tissues. They waited anxiously for assistance. Gary said,

"Maria, why didn't you shoot me?"

She said, "My finger was frozen on the trigger. I tried to pull the trigger but couldn't. I thought you were going to kill me".

Ballistic tests later proved that the rifle was in good working order. In other words, it wasn't faulty, it could fire. The woman looked at Gary and said,

"I'm a Catholic. I believe in Jesus and when you mentioned His name, I knew then you were telling the truth".

Gary said, "Let's pray right now and thank God. If you had pulled the trigger the next shot would have come from my partner and he would have shot you".

As Gary prayed with her, the woman in a gush of tears begged Jesus to forgive her and she received Christ as Saviour there and then as she was lying on the kitchen floor. Bob closed his eyes in prayer. He wasn't a committed Christian then, but years later gave his life to Christ as well. Sadly, Bob was tragically killed whilst riding his pushbike after he retired.

General duty and witness protection police arrived with the news that the two offenders had been arrested, without further incident, only about one kilometre from the house where Gary was. They were heavily armed.

Gary charged Maria with assault and firearm offences and she was given a 'Good Behaviour Bond' by the magistrate as he believed Maria was under 'duress' when she threatened the detectives. He also mentioned the untidy and unshaven state of the 'police' was a mitigating factor. Gary was never so glad to have a shave and haircut. He didn't want to be mistaken every again!

Maria bravely gave evidence in court against the two offenders from Kings Cross and they received a lengthy gaol sentence for their crimes. Maria gave up being a brothel madam and matured as a Christian. Because of further threats by organised crime figures, Maria moved overseas. Gary was told she is running refuges in Thailand and the Philippines to help young street prostitutes recover. This was another 'U' turn in someone's life with God's help. God's amazing intervention is clear throughout this incident. Gary told me, "I really appreciated how fragile life can be after this. You can be here one minute and gone the next. Don't get me wrong. I don't concentrate on dying; I concentrate on living every precious minute, every precious day in God's presence with Michelle.

"Good on you God!"
Police must have their wits about them, especially when it comes to a response where seconds really count. Gary was called out to a car crash at Taylor's Square, Oxford Street, Sydney, in the early

hours of the morning. As Gary travelled to the scene, police on the spot kept asking for an ETA. It was normal for this request to come to the Rescue Squad every few minutes, but in this case Gary was getting asked for their ETA every 30 seconds or less. They sounded very anxious at the scene. As Gary and the late Sergeant Bill Fahey arrived at the scene of the crash, an ambulance officer physically pulled Gary out of the rescue truck by the overalls as he said in a panic,

"Gaz, the life of an unborn baby is in your hands. We've got a woman in heavy labour and she's trying to give birth. She is a passenger in this car and is trapped with her legs closed together and the baby's caught in the birth canal! We've only got seconds. Hurry! The driver is her husband but he's alright. He was driving her to St Margaret's Hospital in heavy labour to have the baby when he lost control and hit another car. The baby is dying."

The blood drained from Bill and Gary's faces. Their heart rate went up and they went into a cold sweat. This was a heavy responsibility, an unborn child's life. This was a deadline they must keep. They worked faster than they had ever worked before.

All the normal road crash protocols were shoved aside. They put the hydraulic gear and cutters straight in to spread, cut, push metal and plastic aside. There wasn't even time for timber wedges or other stabilising gear. The woman screamed in pain. A doctor and midwife had arrived from the hospital down the road to assist the ambulance officers. Even the doctor was panicking saying,

"Speed it up you rescue blokes, we're losing the fight here."

Gary and Bill went even faster. Their equipment worked overtime. The woman was released in record time. On doctor's orders, they placed her on an ambulance stretcher, beside the damaged car. The medical people desperately started to deliver the child. At one stage, the doctor was going to perform an emergency Caesarean Section but he persisted with normal birth giving her medication to increase the speed and vigour of the uterine contractions. Gary, Bill and others held blankets up around the woman for privacy.

Gary watched on with deep emotion with thoughts racing

through his exhausted mind. He questioned himself as to whether he'd done his job in time. Was he quick enough? Did he fail to get the mother out quickly enough to save the baby's life? Moved with such emotion Gary prayed openly,

"Dear Lord Jesus, please save the life of this unborn child, not for me or its parents, but for your glory. Show us your wonderful presence here tonight. In Jesus' name Amen".

Shortly after, Gary and Bill watched the birth of the baby boy. He was a deep purple/grey colour with no signs of breathing or crying. The medics worked hard. For one second, Gary thought he may be dead. Was his faith wavering?

Suddenly the night air was pierced with the baby's first crackly cry. They sucked out the baby's airway and he began to cry loudly and strongly. The doctor looked at Gary and gave the thumbs up. Everyone at the scene yelled with delight and applauded. Gary full of joy prayed aloud again,

"Thank you Jesus for preserving the life of this little boy. You are glorified Lord".

At this time an outlaw biker on his Harley Davidson who had been stopped by police with the rest of the traffic, yelled out in a gruff voice,

"Good on ya God for saving the little brat's life".

Everyone laughed. What a relief as Gary and Bill saw the ambulance drive off to the hospital.

"That was a close one Gaz. Thanks for your prayer", Bill said with emotion.

Gary replied, "You're right mate, we don't want too many more of them. Thankfully God knew what He was doing".

Gary went home to bed and waited for the next call out. He slept 'like a baby' the rest of that early morning. Later in the day Gary and Bill were ordered to attend the hospital for a media conference. Cameras flashed and rolled. Gary and Bill had their photos taken with father, mother and newborn. Gary was instrumental in saving the baby's life by his quick actions. The mother said,

"I want to name my baby boy after you. What's your name?"

"Gary", he said proudly.

"Oh no, I don't like that name".

Everyone laughed. Gary said with a big smile,

"That's alright, I'm sure you'll come up with a better name than Gary".

She eventually called him Damian, who years later, joined the NSW Police Force. Gary wonders if Damian will become a member of the Police Rescue Squad and rescue others, like he rescued him.

"Wrestle in a Chemist Shop"

At a time when Gary was a Detective at Blacktown Police Station he was living at Prospect. One morning Gary was on his way to work when the bus he travelled in came over a hill. He happened to look out of the bus window and saw a man walking along the footpath. Gary recognised the offender who was wanted for an Armed Robbery. They had been after him for a long time. He thought,

"I've got to arrest this fellow but I can't wait until the next bus stop".

Much to the amusement of his fellow passengers, Gary crouched down hiding from the wanted man and shuffled to the front of the bus. Gary said to 'Hank the Yank', the nickname of the driver,

"Stop the bus and open the door when I tell you".

Hank knew Gary was a detective.

Hank asked, "What for?"

"Don't ask questions, just do it!" Gary said forcefully.

Being military trained, a former US Marine, Hank knew how to obey an order and he trusted Gary. Gary crouched down beside the driver and said to Hank,

"Mind my bag I'll get it later".

Hank looked at Gary with a strange look. Gary said,

"That bloke with ginger hair walking down the footpath is wanted. I've got to get the jump on him in case he's armed".

The other passengers were totally perplexed as they stared at Gary's antics. The bus slowed. Gary said,

"Now!"

Hank opened the door. Gary leapt out of the bus. At that split second the offender turned round and saw Gary in mid air. Gary landed on the ground with his hands on the offenders shoulders and brought him to the ground. The man twisted his body and pulled away from Gary's grip. Gary was just a tad too slow with his exit from the bus. The suspect ran down the footpath with Gary in pursuit. The man ran into a chemist shop just as the female shop assistant was unlocking the front door to start work. The suspect slowed down looking for a direction to run inside the shop. Obviously he was looking for the back door.

Gary, who was close behind, jumped and tackled him bringing him to his knees and then the floor. The man twisted his body around facing Gary and they engaged in a wrestle, with the offender trying to get up off the floor and Gary trying to hold him down and turn him back over. Both men were trying to get a better grip using their legs. The trouble was both men were slipping around the floor. As the men fought, fixtures full of pharmacy products were pushed over. There were loud noises of smashing glass, metal and plastic products being dropped as shelves fell to the floor. The two started to roll across the floor in an embrace causing further damage with more fixtures displaced or knocked over. At this time the female shop assistant was screaming loudly,

"Get out or I'll call the police".

Gary yelled to the screaming shop assistant,

"I am the police. Ring triple zero and get police back up immediately!"

The girl stood behind the counter, still screaming. Gary yelled,

"Go on, do it now!"

Then straddling the suspect with his legs and holding the offender with one hand, Gary got his wallet out and threw it to the girl saying,

"My police badge is in my wallet. Ring now".

As Gary turned the offender over, he rammed his arm up his back and wrist locked him. The offender was restrained and gave up. He begged Gary to loosen his grip, but Gary was not going to fall for that old trick. Both were exhausted. Gary then heard police sirens in the distance. Someone else had evidently seen the struggle and called triple zero. Uniformed police and detectives quickly arrived. The offender was searched, handcuffed and there was relief for Gary when they discovered he was unarmed. The man was taken to Blacktown Police Station.

Hank kindly dropped Gary's bag off at the police station. As for the offender, detectives travelled from Sydney City Police Station to interview the offender who was charged with committing a number of armed robberies both in the city and Blacktown. About an hour later, the Chief of Detectives stepped out of his office, pointed to four detectives including Gary and said,

"You, you, you and you, come with me".

Gary was ready for the sergeant's pat on the back for a job well done, but that wasn't the case. The sergeant put them all in police cars and went back to the chemist shop. They were assigned to help chemist shop staff clean up the mess that Gary and the offender had created. The team was there most of the day re packing shelves back to their original state. Fortunately for the chemist, insurance covered any loss due to the fight.

The next morning when Gary boarded the bus for his journey to work he said,

"Good morning Hank".

"Good morning Mr Raymond. Are we going straight to work today?"

"Hank, you just drive the bus, I'll do the rest".

Hank smirked and said,

"I'm thinking of getting a blue light and a siren on the bus if that helps us".

Gary said,

"No but if you can get the word out to all the criminals it's not safe to walk along a bus route in Blacktown, that would be good".

Everybody on the bus laughed. Gary explained what had happened the previous day and for everyone on the bus it was a great source of amusement, but just the same, they were very proud of Gary's brave effort as were his police bosses. The offender was convicted on all counts and received a very hefty sentence. Gary continued to scan the streets from the bus on his way to work and back home.

"Just habit", Gary said.

"Vented Anger"

While he was a detective, Gary decided to get out of the office for a while and grab a coffee, sandwich and newspaper as a relief from an intense morning investigating a child sexual assault. Down he went from the Blacktown Police Station to the local newsagent and bought a paper. Next he went into his favourite coffee shop where he noted there were about half a dozen customers having a pleasant break and chatting away with each other. As he sat down with his coffee Gary noticed a fellow of about forty five years of age with a hamburger on his plate which had not been eaten. He just stared at Gary. Gary didn't make direct eye contact. He scanned his paper but kept a casual eye on the man. He looked 'strange' and somewhat detached. Gary couldn't place him as being known by the police for crime.

Suddenly, without warning, Gary heard a chair loudly scrape across the floor. Gary's table jolted. The man was in front of him with a punch heading towards Gary's face. Fortunately Gary was quick and moved his head sideways. The punch missed. Gary soon had the man in a wrist lock, stood up and thrust the man onto the floor face down and arm barred him. At the same time he yelled,

"I'm a police officer you're under arrest. Don't move! Do you understand I'm a police officer?"

Gary handcuffed him. The man said nothing and didn't resist. Gary directed the shop owner to ring triple zero and tell them a police officer required assistance. The man became upset and began to cry. Gary asked the man for his name and said,

"I'm not going to hurt you, just cooperate. Remember, you're under arrest".

He stood him up and did a search of his pockets. When he looked in the wallet, he discovered the man was on a war pension. He was also a Vietnam veteran and on depression medication. Just then Gary heard police sirens. Two young uniformed police officers walked in and assisted Gary.

Back at Blacktown Police Station Gary cautioned the man and asked him,

"Do you remember what you did?"

"I didn't like the look of you. I thought you were a colonel in the US Army I'd met in Vietnam".

"Did you know I was a police officer?"

"No, please forgive me."

"Of course I forgive you. I'll try and help you if I can, but I still have to charge you. We'll get you to hospital for a mental health check. You caused me a lot of grief, but I'm over it now".

Gary reflected on the incident. There'd been nothing suspicious about the man at first. He'd been dressed in normal casual clothes and appeared to be having lunch. However, Gary found out the man suffered from Post Traumatic Stress Disorder (PTSD) after coming back from the Vietnam War. He told Gary whilst in Vietnam; he'd seen young children napalmed by the US Air Force. When he saw Gary, he reminded him of the US Army Officer in Vietnam. Gary realised the man was delusional and suffering a mental health condition. When he low on medication, he became very angry and confused. When he attacked Gary, he thought he was going to order a napalm strike on civilians and the man had to stop him killing children no matter what. Gary's tidy appearance, hair style and his police demeanour unknowingly set the man off. Not having taken his medication, he was in a psychotic state. Gary told me it was just as well he didn't have a weapon and that he didn't tackle someone else who couldn't defend themselves. Gary gave the man a coffee and spoke with him further. Gary washed his face with cool water as the vet was sweating profusely. Gary prayed with him and charged him with common assault. Shortly after that, the Mental Health Team from Blacktown Hospital arrived to assess the man before going to court. Apparently, full medication containers were found in his bag, indicating he hadn't taken his medication. This probably accounted for his psychotic behaviour.

When in court, the man was asked by the Magistrate,

"Where is your legal representative?" The man pointed straight at Gary and said,

"There he is. He'll help me. I didn't like that other man they sent me (Legal Aid solicitor)". The Magistrate said,

"No that's the arresting police officer. He can't represent you".

"But he was so kind to me, even after I tried to hit him. I want him to speak for me". "You don't understand Sir; Detective Sergeant Raymond is a police officer not a solicitor. You need a legal representative to put submissions to me on your behalf". "No, I want him (again pointing to Gary). I trust him; he's been helping me in the police station. The magistrate looked at Gary and the police prosecutor with a smile and said,

"We'll have a short adjournment so that you can explain the process and get a Legal Aid solicitor for this defendant". The Magistrate added,

"Detective Sergeant Raymond, I see you've been doing your magic again". "Yes Your Worship, I guess so," Gary said, shrugging his shoulders with a grin.

It was well known that Gary, as a Christian cop, calmed many people down when they were agitated. He was occasionally nicknamed 'The People Whisperer' by his fellow police officers.

Gary says,

"When I became a committed Christian, I didn't become a soft touch as some may have thought. I could still handle myself well in a fight and can be 'hard as nails' when I have to be. But I gained a new sense of knowing why people are agitated. Many were just scared, outraged or confused, unaware of what was happening to them during and after their arrest. Some tested you out just to press your buttons and watch your response. Some had deep seated past traumas and acted out like children in trouble. Many were drunk or drugged. Often my patience and negotiation methods prevented a person from causing a situation to escalate between them and the police. No one got hurt. I've even had people confess or make admissions about their crimes just because I treated them kindly. I'm sure some of my colleagues became a bit impatient with my 'whisperings' but it worked most times. I've actually prayed with upset people and have seen them end up in tears as they sensed God was available to help them in their darkest hour, not only them but me as well".

The man who tried to hit Gary was found a Legal Aid representative that he accepted. He was remanded to the Mental Health Unit and received no penalty for the common assault. He is medicated and in an improved state. Gary still sees him from time to time around shopping centres and encourages him to achieve his goals, despite his condition.

"The Meat Cleaver Man"

The streets of Cabramatta, west of Sydney, were extremely dangerous at the height of the drug trafficking era. Methods of passing on drugs were, to say the least, most unhygienic let alone the normal risks involved in drug trafficking. At that time, drug dealers stored heroin in small water balloons which they kept hidden in their mouth under their tongue. If police approached, the dealers or users would swallow those balloons. After police left they would drink copious amounts of water, stick their fingers down their throat and vomit them. Others would retrieve them from the toilet after they passed them in their faeces. They would wash them, place them back in their mouth and sell or use them. It was extremely unhygienic due to the danger of dangerous bacteria or viruses and deadly if the balloon broke in the mouth or stomach. The balloons were the size of a marble and were worth $20 to $40, depending on purity. Money was exchanged and the dealer would spit out a balloon into the hand of a drug user or even onto the ground. The drug user would either put the balloon in their mouth or in their pocket. They would then go to a storm water drain, abandoned building, public toilet, bus, train, car park or even in the middle of a public shopping space to shoot up.

The ground around Cabramatta at that time was heavily littered with used needles and syringes. Ambulances were busy all day and night attending drug overdoses. Police also attended as the risk of violence hung over the heads of the paramedics. They would inject an overdose patient with 'Narcan'. This quickly reversed the effects of the opiate, causing the person to wake up confused and combatative and often requiring restraint by police. It also caused a sort of sudden 'drug withdrawal' which didn't make the addict feel too well, given the money they'd spent on the hit. They often relapsed if not treated again. Gary said,

"We'd often find addicts on the 'nod' or 'asleep' with the needle and syringe still hanging out of their arm or another injection site. Some were nearly asleep on their feet. I don't know how they didn't fall over. I saw one bloke asleep while sitting upright on a park bench still holding a milkshake with the straw still in his mouth. It was sad as it reminded me of a young child falling to sleep in its high chair during its feed. When I woke him to check his level of consciousness, he dropped his milkshake. He was very upset so I bought him another one which calmed him down.

People used to ask me,

"What police station do you work at?" I would reply,

"The streets of San Fran Cabramatta", like the saying on the old TV show 'The Streets of San Francisco'. It was tragic to see people not only ruining their lives, but their families as well. The drugs started as a thrill for them but ended up as being vital medication to keep their entire mind, body and soul in a state of sedation. Other drugs, like the amphetamines, caused a state of continuous 'go, go, go'. Some would stay awake for three days. Many died, many went mad and many went to gaol. Off duty, I mixed with normal people which were like a God given reminder to me that, not all the world is a mess like Cabramatta was at that time. Cabramatta is far better today. Off duty, family and friends would laugh with me, but working in Cabramatta at the time was no laughing matter".

To add to Cabramatta's troubles, there were dangerous disputes between drug dealers and drug users. On one occasion, two dealers argued over money and territory. One shot the other in both knees with a small calibre pistol. The police call it, kneecapping. The shooter ran away. The ambulance took the injured dealer to hospital, escorted by armed police in case another attempt was made to shoot him. The man went through a great deal of pain but refused to give police any information about who shot him. However the detectives involved knew well from experience that there'd be a payback time. Police couldn't act, the 'streets' weren't talking. The police are seriously restrained by the 'code of silence'. About a year later the dealer who'd been shot in the knees saw the dealer who'd shot him sitting on a bus seat in Cabramatta. He was dealing 'heroin balloons' from his mouth. The 'shot in the knee caps' dealer obviously saw this as payback time. Because of the Knife Legislation, gangs stopped carrying knives however; they hid them all over the place. They would hide them in leaf litter, in tree branches, under garbage containers, up drain pipes, in guttering, taped under seats and many more concealed places.

This man ran into a restaurant, past the customers sitting at tables and into the kitchen. Glancing around, he saw a meat cleaver, grabbed it from its food chopping board and raced back through the restaurant back to the street. He snuck up to the bus seat behind the dealer and viciously struck him in the side of the neck with the cleaver. He got away on foot.

The damage was so bad it was amazing that the man's head didn't fall off. Perhaps it would have if it had not been a glancing blow. The wounded man slumped screaming onto the seat bleeding profusely. When the drug users on the street saw what had happened, they raced to the wounded man and put their fingers into his mouth and fished out the heroin balloons for themselves whilst blood spurted everywhere. Covered in blood they ran off leaving the dealer to bleed to death, only caring about their 'precious heroin'. On his way to the scene, Gary told the police, which had arrived at the dealer, to stop the massive bleeding by applying direct pressure to the wound. They did their best. At the scene, Gary's ambulance experience again came to the fore. He took over with gloved hands, reaching into the wound and pinching off the carotid artery and jugular vein lacerations on the heart side. It was effective. Gary, seeing the amount of blood splattered everywhere and the terrified look in the dealer's eyes, prayed out aloud and asked God to help preserve the man's life.

Ambulance officers arrived and took over the fight for the dealer's life. The wounded dealer went straight to hospital and was immediately operated on by specialist surgeons who saved his life by a whisker.

A week later, Gary saw the man in hospital. In tears he said to Gary,

"Please thank everybody who saved my life sir. I thought I was going to die when I became dizzy and couldn't breathe properly. My heart was thumping in my chest a million miles an hour. I heard you praying and told God in my head, that if I survived this, I would do anything for Him. I still can't believe I'm alive." Gary said with a grin,

"Mate, can I tell you it's a miracle that you survived that chop to the neck. Only God could have done that, not me, not the ambos and not the surgeons. I know God used all of us to help you, but in the end, it's His decision whether you live or die." Staring at Gary he was crying even more vigorously when he said,

"How do I keep my promise to God, Mr Raymond?" Gary said,

"Well I've got a Bible here for you. In the back are the steps to salvation. Read them and do it. Don't ever turn back to that garbage you've been involved in. God has an incredible plan for you mate." Gary prayed with him and left.

Weeks later the man came to see Gary. He was neat, well dressed and looked well. He showed Gary the massive scar on his neck which was healing well, although still red around the edges. He told Gary he'd made a full commitment to Christ. He'd left drug dealing and was still in drug rehabilitation getting clean. He was attending church and had joined a Bible study. He said to Gary,

"Someone at church told me, that even though I don't know my future, I know who holds my future." Gary said,

"Yes mate, your scar reminds me that Jesus was scarred for us on the cross. His hands and feet give us that reminder. Jesus in glory still bears those scars". Gary keeps in touch with his new mate from time to time who is now totally off drugs and doing youth ministry. Gary says,

"What we mess up, God fixes up, if we let Him".

The former dealer's assailant could not be identified by his victim as he approached from behind. And again, the 'code of silence' by witnesses was alive and well so the assailant could not be brought to justice. Gary's mate confessed to his shooting however, the victim left the Australia and went back to Vietnam. He would not return to answer for his crime or give evidence in others.

"There have been a number of these types of incidences in Cabramatta involving cleavers, knives and even swords in street brawls during the 'bad old days'. Many police have 'cutting weapon' stories from that era" The throat or chest seems to be the popular target areas. They produce particularly bad wounds, often causing death or permanent disabilities. I often saw victims lose most of their blood volume, puncture their lungs, slash their bowel, break their bones, lose their spleen and lose muscles. Dealers and gang members sometimes cut users' faces with razor blades if they don't pay back drug debts. Young female addicts not only had their faces slashed, but their breasts too. Often heterosexual or homosexual prostitution was a big part of the drug landscape. Extortion was rife in Cabramatta until police closed down the 5T Gang after John Newman's assassination. Today Cabramatta is a great Asian precinct which is safe and vibrant. It is well worth the visit. They have great noodle soups, the best I've tasted", Gary exclaimed.

"Rifle in the Back of a Car"

Gary and his mate returned to the station after a rescue mission. Gary alighted from the rescue truck to stop traffic whilst the truck was backed into the station from a nearby lane. No traffic was in sight, so Gary indicated to the driver that it was safe to back onto the roadway from the laneway and into the station. As the truck backed up it blocked the road. As they did this manoeuvre, suddenly a car screeched around the corner at incredible speed. Gary had to jump out of the way. The car swerved toward the truck and shuddered to a standstill. Gary ran to the driver's door angrily. Just as he was about to give the man at the wheel a mouthful of good advice, he saw a sawn off rifle on the back seat partially covered by a bath towel.

Gary held his breath in shock and fear. He lunged forward, quickly covered the man's eyes with one hand and grabbed the ignition keys with the other and threw them onto the road. The driver tried to open the passenger's door and get away. Gary reached in, struck him on the tip of the jaw with his fist and at the same time held the man's clothing. He pulled him out of the car onto the roadway and restrained him. Gary's partner stepped out of the truck confused and wondering what Gary was doing. Gary yelled,

"There's a gun on the back seat".

His mate helped to restrain the man on the road. A number of other rescue police came out to see what the fuss was about. At that very same moment, a voice came over the Police Radio Room telling all cars to keep a look out for an armed robber with a sawn off rifle who'd committed a robbery in the area. They gave out a description. Surprised, Gary realised the man he had in custody matched the description perfectly. Gary feeling very proud and a little amused yelled,

"Hey guys, tell VKG we have the suspect in custody, the gun and the money is secure".

The police on the radio couldn't believe their ears. Was this the rescue squad arresting armed robbers? Gary didn't tell them the suspect literally drove into his arms, like a fish jumping into a fishing boat. This was a case of the robber coming to Gary rather than Gary going to a robber. It was an easy catch. Gary and his mates had a good joke at the robber's expense.

All jokes aside, the potential for harm to Gary and his mate had been great had Gary not noticed the gun on the back seat. It's not unusual for police to be thrust into a situation without notice and have to act on their tactical and survival skills. Gary calls it, "seconds to think". Desperate men do desperate things to escape going to gaol. Gary could have been shot or run over, but on this occasion like many others, God's protection was upon him. Most times things turn out for the best in the art of crime stopping. Literally caught in the act, the offender pleaded guilty and was sentenced to seven years in gaol.

"Murder Prevented"

Gary was living in Fairfield, a Sydney south western suburb and on call. About 3.00am he received a call to attend a motor vehicle collision where people were trapped. The rescue truck was in his driveway at home. Gary travelled down the Horsley Drive towards the scene of the crash with his vehicle's revolving roof lights activated. He didn't bother using his siren as it was early hours of the morning. As he drove, he noticed the bright lights of a vehicle coming towards him. The car drew closer and the driver, without warning, suddenly turned right in front of Gary's rescue truck. Both vehicles collided with a huge deep bang. There wasn't even enough time to brake. Gary noticed that the driver of the car was being tossed about because he wasn't wearing a seat belt. He watched the driver's head whip around forwards, backwards and sideways. It slammed into the roof and steering wheel. There were no air bags in those days.

The vehicles came to rest with dust filling the air. Gary was shocked, but called on his radio for urgent ambulance and police assistance. He thought the man was going to die. Gary was extremely shaken, not injured and climbed out of his caved in rescue truck. The driver had turned into a driveway in front of Gary. Then he saw what appeared to be smoke, so Gary hurriedly grabbed a fire extinguisher from his truck. Thankfully, it turned out to be steam from the damaged cooling system. The driver was unconscious. Grabbing a cervical collar from his first aid kit, Gary placed it around the man's neck; inserted an airway into his mouth and an oxygen therapy mask on his face. A crowd gathered. An off duty nurse who was woken from her sleep assisted. Time seemed to stop for Gary. He then noticed blood coming out of the driver's left ear and from his nose. This suggested an injury at the base of his skull.

Gary kept the man's neck straight, and with the help of bystanders, 'log rolled' the driver to drain blood from the airway and ear. There was no other blood visible, but the right shoulder was dislocated and the man's chest rattled. Gary realised there was a strong possibly he had a closed chest injury as well. Gary prayed with him, believing he was going to die.

Waiting for help, Gary looked around the inside of the car; he noticed a baby seat in the back. Fortunately it was empty, but he had a look around in case a baby had gone under or between the seats. Gary had seen this happen in previous rescues with unrestrained children. As he searched the car, another shock was coming. Gary found a loaded .22 calibre rifle under the front seat. Ambulance and police officers arrived and took over. Other police rescue and ambulance personnel had been dispatched to the original collision Gary was going to. After ambulance checks and a breath test by the supervising sergeant, Gary was taken back to Fairfield Police Station to be interviewed by investigators and complete a statement. Later, the truth came out.

It was revealed the man had found out his wife was in bed with her lover at a block of units on the Horsley Drive, Fairfield. The man enraged with revenge, thankfully left his three children at home and went off intending to kill his wife and her lover with the gun in the car. When he recovered in hospital some six months later, he was charged with a number of offences and received a gaol term. Who knows what happened to his kids? Gary breathed a sigh of relief when he realised that, inadvertently he had prevented a double murder by just driving down the road. The man had been so angry and full of resentment he'd wrecked his chance of killing his wife and her lover by turning in front of Gary's vehicle.

Gary still wonders why he was so 'locked out' of his senses that he didn't notice the flashing lights on Gary's police rescue vehicle. I guess that's what happens when people are in such a rage. It is just their little world at the time – who cares about anyone else? Through his anger he lost control of the car. It was surely a case of 'an ill wind that blows well'. For Gary, he was used to rescuing people from car crashes, but not involved in one himself. It's a lot more stressful to be there on the spot than to turn up after the impact is all over, like Gary normally did. Gary told me,

"I had a few nightmares after that. I kept recalling the driver's head bashing around on impact. I was also very wary of approaching vehicles for a while, scared they might turn into me. I'm right now of course, but it was a challenge for a while".

CHAPTER ELEVEN

THE WRAP UP
AND TALE ENDER

Like the hymn writer John Newton, Gary Raymond has 'come through many dangers, toils and snares'. He learned the power of a disciplined life early and this discipline followed through during his police service. He is also an exact person. I gained official permission to ride along with Gary in the police car to get to know him better in preparation for this book. One day when I was with him, a woman cut in front of us going at a pace. Gary pulled her over. She said she'd gone a 'little' over speed to get her son to a birthday party. Gary looked at her and said,

"Madam, speeding is speeding, a little or a lot is still speeding. Slow down unless you want your son in the city mortuary instead of a birthday party."

The women understood the message loud and clear with Gary giving it to her straight. Gary took her details down in his police notebook. She cried and promised to slow down. Gary believes in the authority of a loving, yet just God and says, "

Here is the whole conclusion of the matter:

'*Fear God and keep his commandments for this is the whole duty of man.*' *(Ecclesiastes 12:13 NIV).*

However, he'd add that the Christian's task is to go further, as Saint Peter advised, '*Grow in the grace and knowledge of our Lord and Saviour Jesus Christ.' (2 Peter 3:18 NIV)*

Gary told me, "I look forward to seeing Jesus face to face one day, either at my death or at Jesus promised return".

There's More, Far More...

There are many other situations that involved Gary. One book alone could not even begin to contain the many adventures of Gary Raymond. It would take several. At least this book will wet the appetite of those interested in more.

SUICIDE AWARENESS

∽

As an ambulance officer and police officer, Gary has gained vast experience dealing with suicide. One of his missions in life is to contribute to the reduction of suicide in the world. Suicide claims the lives of over 2,000 Australians each year. More people die by suicide than in car crashes. For every person who dies, there are another eleven people who are directly affected. This means that suicide impacts the lives of over 22,000 Australians each year. The grief, confusion and anguish that comes from losing someone you love, a family member, friend, colleague or entertainer is devastating. Gary provides advice gathered from years of experience in dealing with those who consider taking their life.

WHAT ARE THE AUSTRALIAN SUICIDE STATISTICS?

- There were 2,191 deaths from suicide registered in 2008. This has risen from 1,799 recorded in 2006.
- 78% of suicides were males.
- In 2008, intentional self-harm was ranked as the 14th leading cause of all deaths registered in Australia.
- Males accounted for over three quarters of all suicide deaths in 2008, resulting in a ranking as the 10th leading cause of death

for males.

- In 2008, the most frequent method of suicide was hanging, a method used in over half (53%) of all suicide deaths. Poisoning by drugs was used in 12% of suicide deaths, followed by poisoning and other methods including by alcohol and motor vehicle exhaust 11%. Methods using firearms accounted for 7.8% of suicide deaths. The remaining suicide deaths included deaths from drowning, jumping from a high place and others.

WHAT ARE THE HIGH RISK GROUPS?

Gary says some of the high risk groups for suicide are:-

- people who have previously attempted suicide
- people who have lost someone significant like a spouse, parent or sibling
- those who have lost a role model, like a pop star or sports star
- those copying a close friend's suicide (contagion effect)
- depressed caring professionals like doctors, dentists, nurses, psychologists, counsellors, social workers, police officers, ambulance officers, fire fighters, rescue squads (these all include both paid employees and unpaid volunteers)
- depressed or confused mentally ill people
- victims of abuse or neglect
- victims of bullying
- people in dysfunctional or broken relationships
- homosexuals and gender confused people (cross dressers, cross gender etc)
- people with financial loss, financial mismanagement or gamblers
- alcohol or substance abusers
- those depressed by inappropriate prescribing or misuse of behavioural medications
- depressed senior citizens
- those fearing failure or failure to achieve a goal or vision
- people associated with the occult or involved in a cult (may be multiple suicides)
- Australia's indigenous people
- people in custody under police, mental health, immigration or

corrective services
- young men under 25 years
- people with sacrificial ideology (suicide bombers or domestic violence offenders)
- people who decide to 'suicide by police' (those who confront police deliberately with weapons)
- people who barricade themselves or take hostages
- depressed terminally ill or permanently incapacitated people (euthanasia is suicide)
- depressed defence force or former defence personnel (in peacetime or combat)
- people involved in an overwhelming critical incident or natural disaster
- people suffering Post Traumatic Stress Disorder (PTSD)
- depressed children of Vietnam, Iraq or Afghanistan war veterans
- depressed rural residents (drought, flood losses)
- any sudden traumatic loss or change in a person's life
- people who feel victimised after a perceived injustice, personal or emotional hurt (may be self pity, vindictive or payback suicide)
- people with a manipulative personality who become depressed
- people being treated for a mental illness in a psychiatric facility, or who have been recently discharged from an institution

HOW DO YOU PREVENT SUICIDE?

Gary next asks a vital question, "What outward signs and symptoms will you **first** notice when looking for suicidal people?" The answer is surprising at first. "Usually **none**," Gary answers. A circumstance, such as a depressing loss or change, is the first suicide risk potential indicator. Signs and symptoms come later as their circumstances fail to resolve and people fail to cope.

Chronic or acute depression in people is also an early indicator of a suicide risk as well. It may be brain dysfunction, head injury, medication, depressing circumstances or all of them.

Gary explains that it's very important to keep an eye out for **sudden unexplained improvement** in a person during or after depression. It may mean they have actually decided to suicide. They develop a 'false peace' because they have finally made the decision to suicide and have an eerie calm about it. They may express hopelessness and helplessness with their life.

WHAT ARE THE SIGNS OF SUICIDE RISK?

Gary lists a number of signs of those who may be a suicide risk whilst depressed:-

- previous suicide attempts or self inflicted injuries
- noticeable changes in people's behaviour and personality
- depressed people who finalise business, employment, bank, investment etc.
- people who give away personal and valuable things
- people who sell sentimental or valuable things cheaply
- people who visit or contact relatives and friends to say goodbye
- people who make a will or arrange their funeral whilst depressed
- people who take out substantial life insurance whilst depressed
- people who avoid holidays, social outings with family and friends
- people who become a loner, secretive or locking themselves away
- people who engage in death talk, general departure talk or death fantasies
- people who joke or use 'throw off' lines about their suicide
- people who may see a doctor without being sick to falsely obtain medication for suicide, such as sleeping pills or sedatives
- people who purchase poisonous products for no legitimate reason
- people who take time off work, truant from school, or avoid education and training commitments.
- people who obtain a gun, bring one out of storage, access military, police force or sporting weapons
- people who are depressed who change their normal habits or routines
- people who engage in out of character sexual behaviour
- people who are more interested in life after death issues and funerals

- people who have anger outbursts or, conversely, passive aggressive behaviour (they sulk or are non compliant)
- people who enquire about means and methods of how to die
- people who express unmanageable grief or trauma over a loss or change
- people who display suicide methods in rituals, or perform suicide rehearsals
- people who visit and check out a suicide location (reconnaissance)
- people who develop eating or sleeping disorders
- people who become obsessive about anything
- people who behave recklessly or negligently (driving or extreme sports, etc)
- people who avoid organisational commitments and neglect their team

All of these signs can either manifest alone or in clusters. Gary passionately conveys the message that the best way to find out if a person is suicidal is to **'ask'** them. Do it openly and gently as part of your normal conversation with that depressed person. The question to use is, **"Are you suicidal?"**

While that might seem a little direct, directness means openness, and that is what a suicidal person is looking for during their struggle with suicidal thoughts and feelings. Avoidance by a carer erodes confidence in the carer's ability to relate openly and honestly to the suicidal person without fear or embarrassment.

How do you find out how deeply depressed they are? Gary says to ask using a quantitative measure. "On a scale of 1 to 10, where 1 is, 'I feel a little bit down' and 10 is 'I am devastated.' This will show how they feel about themselves. If we don't do this, the carer may misjudge the situation. Remember, 'don't judge a book by its cover.' Asking them on the scale is a 'self assessment' by the depressed person of themselves, and is generally more accurate. If they are intoxicated or psychotic, it may not work accurately, but it is still wise to ask."

Later, we can use the same measurement scale to assess our

progress as we give ongoing support. We can ask, "You said you were a nine this morning. What are you now?" Whatever number they give will help you measure the progress of support, whether they are better or worse. To further explore you can ask, "What has changed your number?" This will indicate what support strategies are working and what's not.

Gary says that once a person reveals they are suicidal, here are more questions to gently ask. Ask them if they have a 'plan'. Talk about the plan. Use the 'How, When, Where and Why' questions:-

1. **How** are they going to suicide? (don't presume the method)
2. **When** are they going to suicide? (don't presume the time)
3. **Where** are they going to suicide? (don't presume the place)
4. **Why** are they going to suicide? (don't presume the reason)

Gary says that many people are afraid that if they ask a person, "Are you suicidal?" and they're not suicidal, that they will lose a friend? The answer is "No." People appreciate your care and personal concern. He says that if they're not suicidal at that time in their depression, it will give them a future invitation, just in case. He also says that we should believe them up front and not call them a liar or accuse them of holding back their true feelings from you.

WHAT IS A FUTURE INVITATION?

The future invitation is an offer to support someone who may become suicidal in the future. It goes like this, "You said you're not suicidal after this loss. I believe you however, if you do happen to feel suicidal at any time in the future, promise you'll call me immediately and I'll get some support for you." The future invitation shows a deep level of care. Just explain, "I brought up the subject of suicide, because I know that some depressed people get suicidal. I care enough about you to ask you about suicide, if it means saving your life. You're special to me."

This is a reminder from Gary about one of the great suicide myths: that asking about suicide will give them the idea. It won't give them the idea. Talking about suicide does not make someone suicidal, but it opens discussion on what they are already thinking or planning.

WHY SUICIDE AWARENESS EDUCATION?

Research proves that receiving 'Suicide Awareness Education' and applying it reduces the incidence of suicide in the community. One of the biggest dangers in dealing with a suicidal person is to not believe them. One of the most vulnerable times for suicidal people is the time between interventions. That is after hospital stays, psychiatrist or psychologist appointments or during outpatient programs.

WHAT IS THE SUICIDAL & HOMICIDAL RELATIONSHIP?

Another huge lesson for carers is to realise that **homicidal** people may become **suicidal**, and **suicidal** people may become **homicidal.** This becomes a safety and security issue for all involved. Psychotic mentally ill patients may become suicidal and homicidal. There are also those in domestic disputes, or terrorists. Victims of bullying are a high risk group for turning homicidal and suicidal. Carers should be careful. If people are violent, call the police on the emergency number for your country.

WHAT ARE THE SUICIDE MYTHS?

Gary emphasises that there are many myths when it comes to suicide. He mentions some in a True or False format:-

Myth: Most suicides occur during a full moon.
False: This myth is not supported by research, although night time is a significant time when some depressed people are alone or under less scrutiny from others.

Myth: People who suicide are mentally ill.
False: Most people who suicide have never been diagnosed with a psychiatric illness however, people with mental illness are a very high risk group.

Myth: Teenagers tell their peers before their family about their suicide thoughts or plans.

True: Yes they do. Teenagers talk to other teenagers about teen issues including parents, school, marriage, study, career, money, drugs, sex, music, fashion and suicide.

Myth: People who threaten suicide want attention.
False: People who threaten suicide don't want attention, they **need** attention.

Myth: People who are suicidal always tell their family.
False: Families are the least likely to be told.

Myth: People who talk, write or threaten suicide won't really do it. They are just attention seeking.
False: Talking, writing or threatening suicide is an indication of a serious plea for help and should be responded to immediately. They are a high risk.
Myth: Suicide occurs without warning.
False: 8 out of 10 people give verbal warnings, veiled indicators and display warning signs of their intent to suicide.

Myth: Most suicidal people present indicators.
True: They communicate suicidal intentions in words, writings, actions and inactions.

Myth: It's rare for people to attempt suicide more than once.
False: 4 out of 5 adult suicides have made previous attempts.

Myth: Mentioning suicide to a depressed person gives them the idea.
False: They already have suicidal thoughts and ideas. Mentioning it opens up honest sharing about their suicide struggle or ambivalence.

Myth: Suicidal people are loners.
False: Most suicidal people mix with family, workmates and the community before their suicide. They are ordinary people with

extraordinary problems.

Myth: Suicide is genetic.
False: Research does not support this idea of a 'suicide gene' however, grief driven or 'copy cat' suicides may occur after the death of a significant person in their lives. It's called the 'Contagion Effect'. Some mental illnesses have genetic origins, but not suicide itself.

Myth: If a suicidal person asks you to keep their thoughts, threats or plans a secret, you should abide by their request for confidentiality.
False: You should never keep suicide plans a secret. Negotiate with the suicidal person as to who they prefer for support. Always tell someone who can help, especially people who can offer professional support. If you think it is urgent, call an ambulance or the police without delay.

Myth: Relationship breakups are common throughout your life and shouldn't cause suicidal thoughts.
False: People going through relationship breakups are a suicide high risk group, especially if they were the one who didn't want the breakup to happen.

Myth: Suicidal people want to die.
False: Most suicidal people don't want to die. They just want relief from emotional emptiness, pain, hurt, fear, hopelessness, helplessness, grief or depression.

Myth: Suicide only affects certain types of people with weak personalities.
False: Suicide affects all personality types, the young, old, rich, poor, educated, uneducated, all nationalities and religions.

Myth: Suicide is always impulsive.
False: The majority of suicides are planned. The minority are impulsive and carried out in a momentary crisis, especially influenced by the person being psychotic, drunk or drugged.

Myth: Self mutilation is different behaviour from attempted suicide.
True. However, some self mutilators may go on to complete their suicide deliberately or accidently.

Myth: Suicide can be prevented.
True: Suicide is both detectable and preventable. More people should become 'suicide aware'. Like medical first aid, people need mental health first aid skills.

Myth: A depressing event or circumstance can be the first indicator of a suicide risk.
True: A depressing loss or change in a person's life happens before any signs of suicidal intent emerge. As they fail to cope with the event or change depression may get deeper.

Myth: We should never dare or suggest a person complete suicide.
True. Bluffing, joking, goading or daring someone to suicide may cause vulnerable people to actually follow through with their intentions.

Myth: To attempt suicide is a crime.
False: It is not a criminal offence to attempt or threaten suicide. It is however, a criminal offence to assist someone to suicide.

Myth: Suicide notes or messages are helpful for relatives as they explain the reasons for the death.
False: Most suicide notes are confusing, contradictory and irrational. They may trigger grief, anger and guilt for those left behind.

Myth: Suicidal people may become aggressive.
True: Some suicidal people can be very angry, aggressive and dangerous.

Myth: Suicidal people operate mainly on feelings rather than on rational thinking.
True. Most suicidal people are egocentrical and don't think rationally

about other people when they are suicidal.

Myth: People who joke about their suicide are not serious.
False: People, who talk about their suicide, whether in a depressive or joking manner, must be taken seriously.

Myth: We should just let some hopeless people suicide.
False: Life is a sacred gift. Suicidal people are planning a permanent solution to a temporary problem and should be encouraged to live.

Myth: Vietnam veterans' children are a high risk suicide group.
True. In fact the children of Vietnam veterans have three times the risk of suicide.

Myth: People never make their suicide look like an accident.
False: Some people have been known to suicide on the transport system, at the workplace or at home and plan to make it look like an accident.

Myth: Once suicidal, always suicidal.
False: Many people rise from depression, never again to be suicidal.

Myth: Suicide rates are higher for low income earners.
False: Income does not discriminate in suicide.

Myth: Suicide rates are higher for women than for men.
False: Suicide attempts are higher for women. However suicide completions are higher for men.

Myth: Men use more violent suicide means.
True: Research shows men use more violent means most of the time.
Myth: Suicide rates are higher than homicide rates.
True: Suicide rates are much higher than homicide rates.

Myth: Victims of bullying are a suicide risk.
True. Fear and rejection cause these victims to become a suicide

risk. They may also have homicidal thoughts.

WHAT IS SUICIDE CRISIS NEGOTIATION?
Stopping a suicidal person is not for the fainthearted for it takes training, skill, wisdom and patience. Negotiation is a vital word that means, 'Mutual discussion and arrangement of the terms of a transaction or agreement'. Gary Raymond advises that when dealing with a person threatening immediate suicide, in Australia ring the police and ambulance without delay.

Focus on:-
- retrieval talk not diagnosing
- retrieval talk not counselling
- retrieval talk not therapy
- retrieval talk not idle chatter

Professional support should be carried out in a 'safer place' at a 'safer time'. Gary says sarcastically, "It's not good to have a counselling session with a person threatening suicide at the edge of a cliff, on a bridge, up a tower or on a 30 storey building."

WHAT ARE THE NEGOTIATOR'S ENVIRONMENTS?
Gary says that Suicide Negotiators may have to negotiate in many different environments such as:-

- face to face
- via a third person
- telephone (landline, mobile or satellite)
- text messaging
- mail
- email
- internet chat room
- blog
- two way radio, (government, citizen's band, air traffic, marine etc.)

- using language interpreters or sign language experts

HOW DO YOU PHONE CONNECT TO A SUICIIDAL PERSON?

Gary asks, "What should be one of the first things you say during a suicide crisis negotiation on the phone?" The answer is simple but amazing, "If we lose the connection, it's not me hanging up and terminating your call. Please give me your number or ring me back if that happens." This assures the person that if the phone connection is lost for any reason whatsoever, it's not you either hanging up or dismissing their pleas for help. The suicidal person may take a phone disconnection 'personally as rejection' which is psychologically dangerous. During or after the conversation, don't hang up your phone. Use another phone to ring police for a trace or triangulation on the person's call to be initiated from the Police Communications Centre.

HOW DO YOU APPROACH A SUICIDAL PERSON THREATENING TO JUMP?

Gary informed me that when approaching a person threatening suicide, he stops his approach to stay at a safe distance, especially outside of 'kicking range' or 'leg sweep range' just in case they get aggressive and try to knock him over. Watch they don't grab you in anger and attempt to pull you over the edge with them.

On approach there is the 'alert zone' when the person becomes aware of your presence at the scene. The 'defence zone' is when you may get too close; the person becomes defensive and may threaten you if you don't stop moving forward. Finally, there's the 'attack zone' when the person may engage you physically with or without a weapon. Remember, ordinary objects like nail files, combs, shoes or scissors can be turned into weapons. Many working men carry pocket knives that may be used in anger or fear.

Gary emphasises that, whatever you do, do not try to take or wrestle a weapon from a person. You may be killed or injured in the scuffle. Encourage them to put the weapon down and walk to you, rather than you walk towards an armed person. In any case, urgently escape and call police. Even if you know the person well as a relative or friend, still escape. They may be psychotic, homicidal, uncontrollably angry or fearful. Police and ambulance officers must be called to restrain the person and get them to emergency support.

WHAT ARE FIREARM & CUTTING WEAPON DANGERS?

If the person has a firearm or cutting weapon, there is no alternative but to escape immediately, take cover, and call the police. Warn others around you to escape with you and take cover as well. Avoid approaching any person unless safe to do so. Always have an escape plan if things turn nasty.

Gary advises:
- work out how to escape (your method)
- work out when to escape (your opportunity)
- formulate an escape excuse (your reason)
- work out where to escape to (your place of safety)

If confined, you may only have the opportunity to escape behind a table or into another room. If the person is dangerous to you, put space between you and them. Remember, if you escape to a room, don't just lock the door, '**barricade**' doors and windows using stacked up furniture as well. Don't come out of your safe place until you confirm that police have arrived and have given you a direction that it is safe to come out of your hiding place.

WHAT ARE THE SAFE APPROACH & NEGOTIATION HINTS?

In your approach, Gary says you should do the following:-
- give the person plenty of audible warnings of your approach
- introduce yourself and your purpose
- introduce other carers at the scene
- don't sneak up on them
- approach slowly and give verbal assurance you are there to help and not hurt them

- beware of environmental dangers, such as loose rocks or slippery surfaces
- be willing to retreat and get more help if necessary
- plead with them assertively not to suicide, and plead for time to talk and listen
- point out lethality (dangers) that they may be in at the present
- make an apology for any possible errors you may make in your speech or actions toward them, to assure them that if you make mistakes, they are not intentional
- ask compliance questions like, "What do I have to do, or not do, to prevent your suicide?"
- clear the scene of people who threaten the safety or security of successful negotiations such as aggressive relatives or friends
- quarantine the scene from uninvited intrusions during negotiation by forming perimeters and creating an exclusion zone
- beware of the person's suicide exhibition behaviour like leaning out over the edge, swinging out over the edge, temporarily letting go of handholds, scratching themselves with a knife or taking a small number of tablets
- discourage exhibition behaviour as they may 'accidentally' fall over the edge or cut an artery
- be aware the exhibition behaviour may be a suicide 'rehearsal'
- be gently directive
- assure them you believe their threat
- point out the dangers to them (location lethality)
- point out they may "slip and fall" (behaviour lethality)
- plead with them to keep still
- in your speech, don't be submissive but be assertive without being aggressive

Gary points out that during a negotiation try not to say "if" but "when": "When you come back from the edge we will support you with counselling." 'When' is positive and shows you really believe they will not die and there is hope for their future.

Also during a negotiation try not to say "I" but say "we": "When you come back from the edge we will support you with counselling." This shows that many people are ready and willing to support them.

They are not alone. It is a team effort.

WHAT IS A RETRIVAL PLAN?

A retrieval plan is how you are going to get the suicidal person from their dangerous predicament to safety into the hands of the police, ambulance, mental health team or chaplaincy team. It usually starts with a survival contract. Then you negotiate the retrieval plan with the suicidal person. Discuss the personnel, timing and methods you will use to bring them to a safe and secure place. It's done a little at a time, bit by bit.

HOW DO WE USE A SURVIVAL CONTRACT?

A survival contract is when we ask the suicidal person to contract, promise, agree or undertake not to suicide. This contact is very powerful and gives the person an opportunity to make a decision not to suicide. The contact is reached like this, "I know you're depressed but please promise me you won't suicide." If the person says, "Yes", proceed with your retrieval plan.

If the person says, "No, I can't promise", try to gain a survival contract with a time attached to it. "Well promise me you will not suicide in the next 24 hours." If they say, "Yes", continue the negotiation. Time is valuable. If they say, "No", call for help.

HOW LETHAL IS THE THREAT?

Gary says that negotiators need to assess the lethality of the threat, *i.e.* how deadly the threat really is:-

- what is suicidal person's intent
- what is the suicide location like
- what is the suicide method or means and how deadly is it
- are they threatening suicide verbally, physically or both
- are they unable to control their emotions and actions
- are they staring into space or not communicating
- are they constantly staring at the suicide means
- are they hiding or running away from help

HOW DO YOU VISIT SUICIDAL PEOPLE?

When visiting suicidal people:-
* notify someone, or take someone along with you
* arrange regular updates of your progress by phone
* seek advice until police and ambulance arrive
* ensure you have referral details to professional help if required

HOW DOES THE NEGOTIATOR'S RESPOND?

Gary advises the following strategies:-
* beware of the person's anger level
* be ready for sudden mood changes
* take them seriously and don't ridicule
* don't joke or laugh at their jokes
* don't 'mirror' their behaviour or use bad language
* encourage the person to talk out their homicidal ideation (thoughts) as it helps them to emotionally vent, distracts them from the suicide threat and 'buys' time

Look for evidence of:-
* barricading or hostage taking by the person
* violence against other people or pets
* violence against property
* alternative suicide or homicide means which may be concealed but within reach
* evidence of 'concealment' (hiding themselves, something or someone)
* access to a motor vehicle or other get away transport which could add even more danger to them and the community if they are mobile and out of control

WHAT IS PERTURBATION?

Gary cleverly explains perturbation. He says that perturbation is a term referring to the person's level of disturbance or agitation. How perturbed are they? It's like a thermometer gauging the person's 'emotional temperature'. Are they agitated, annoyed, depressed, in an anxiety state or very calm?

WHAT IS AMBIVALENCE?
Ambivalence is like a pendulum of life and death swinging backwards and forwards in the suicidal person's mind. They are indecisive at this time and going through the following question in their mind over and over again, "Will I or won't I suicide?" Often in their thinking they are confused, delusional, paranoid or emotionally upset. It is the suicide struggle (ambivalence), not the depressive losses or changes that become the issue in the present tense.

They put their problems aside and just concentrate on whether to suicide or not. The carer should make the suicidal person aware that they know about the struggle in their mind that is occurring and invite the person to discuss it openly. We also negotiate the retreat from the edge we call 'de staging'. That means bringing them back from the edge cognitively, physically and emotionally one small step at a time.

WHAT IS THE SECOND AMBILVALENT STRUGGLE?
Sadly, once the person has decided to suicide, they then have the second ambivalent struggle that is, when to suicide. The pendulum in their mind struggles with the right or wrong time to suicide. This is the new big issue for them to decide. Not if I will suicide, but when. We need to find out the significance of the timing, if any. It may be the anniversary of a depressing event or huge loss that's happened to them. It can be more than one event which we call the 'Cumulative Effect.' It's like the 'straw that broke the camel's back.' The present time, date or place might cause them to flashback to the past and become deeply depressed and suicidal.

WHAT IF THE PERSON SETS A DEADLINE?
You may have to intensify the negotiation if a deadline has been set by the person. They may tell you when they're going to carry through with suicide. Ask for the reasons for their deadline and plead for more time. Constantly, but gently attempt to eliminate or extend the deadline. Keep extending the time which will give the person time to change their mind and not suicide. The longer we can

negotiate the more chance of getting them to change their mind and stay alive. Time also helps if they are drunk or drugged. They sober up and become more aware of their danger. It's dangerous at heights if they are too drunk or drugged as they may fall accidently.

Gary said, "In police rescue we often jumped and grabbed people who were too close to the edge to physically retrieve them before they fell. Sometimes we would do it alone or other times with another rescue officer. One would grab the top half of a person and the other, the bottom half. We would drag the person to safety sometimes willingly and other times with a fight. We wore safety harnesses so that we wouldn't go over the side. In all the physical retrievals we did, we didn't lose a single person. Yes risky, but well calculated."

WHAT CAN BE A CRITICAL TIME?
Sunset and sunrise can be a critical time for some suicidal people. Some suicidal people protest, "I can't face another day" or conversely, "I can't face another night." Ascertain if they hate or fear the day or the night. Attempt to retrieve the person before their vulnerable time. Promise support and supervision for their vulnerable time. Attempt to persuade them that the timing is wrong and you do not want them to suicide at any time. As Gary said previously, "Beware of 'sudden unexplained improvement' during a suicide crisis. It may mean a decision to suicide has been made." Ask them about their present thoughts.

WHY USE THE 'PRESENT TENSE' DURING NEGOTIATION?
Gary says it is vital to try and stay in the present tense when negotiating with a suicidal person. Their present circumstance is the most dangerous. The present is changeable but the past is unchangeable with the future unknown. Allow them to talk about the past and future however, keep steering them gently back to the present contract and retrieval plan.

During negotiation, explore the suicidal person's present:-
• thoughts

- emotional feelings
- physical condition
- behavioural moods
- spiritual status

Use caution with sedation or medication whilst on the scene. The suicidal person may already have substances in their body. Prohibit the taking of medication or alcohol during a suicide negotiation as the outcome is too unpredictable and may cause an altered level of consciousness or risky behaviour by the person. They should be medicated at a safer time and placed under medical supervision.

HOW DO WE PHYSICALLY DEAL WITH A NON COMPLIANT PERSON?

- wear personal protection equipment (gloves, eye wear, mask)
- use a proportional number of people to the meet the level of resistance
- use only as much force as necessary when restraining
- don't punish them
- caution with weapons or needle stick injuries from the person
- ensure prevention of injury to all engaged in the struggle
- maintain a clear airway
- apply caution with their breathing
- don't put sustained weight on their throat or chest
- the person may require sedation
- caution from spitting or biting by the person
- use a mental health team or paramedic ambulance transport with police escort

WHAT ARE NON-VERBAL INDICATORS?
When assessing a suicidal person:-
watch their facial expressions
- listen for vocal clues, such as the content and manner of their speech
- watch the person's breathing rate to help monitor emotional

changes and measure perturbation
- their posture, gestures and actions (or inactions) will give you clues
- clothing and grooming (wrong clothes for the weather conditions) will help your assessment
- injuries or illness could mean a previous suicide attempt, previous self mutilation, self abuse, victim of violence or injury whilst on drugs or alcohol

COULD THE PERSON BE WANTED BY THE POLICE?

The suicidal person could even be an offender threatening suicide after committing a criminal act which may be a dangerous situation for the negotiator. The person may run away and hide, or run away to a more dangerous location. They may run away to locate a weapon and return to hurt you or themselves. If they are a fugitive, it may be time for you to enact your escape plan and call the police.

CAN WE BUY TIME?

In most cases, negotiating time decreases perturbation. The longer you can engage a suicidal person in dialogue, the better chance of successful retrieval to professional help. This may also give them time to 'sober up.' In other cases, the longer the time, the more critical the situation becomes as perturbation and lethality may even rise. All negotiations are unique in character. Encourage them to think and talk in 'retrieval time'. If you have to, plead for more time. Discuss the contracts you have made with them, ask them for detail of what's on their mind. Ask them clarifying questions without 'cross examining' them and appear to be prying into their secrets.

WHAT ABOUT PHYSICAL NEEDS?

Use physical needs such as a blanket or drink of water to get them back from the edge. Don't offer hot drinks as they may be dangerous if spilt or thrown. Use location difficulties such as extreme winds, heat, lightning, rain, cold or darkness to convince them to come back. Don't be afraid to tell them you are afraid of the weather conditions and both of you should seek shelter in a safe place.

HOW DO WE DEAL WITH DEMANDS & REQUESTS?

Gary insists the negotiator should not normally initiate demands or offers to the suicidal person. Why? The demands or offers may be unrealistic, unwanted, inappropriate or even harmful. In most cases wait for the suicidal person to make demands or offers. It may come in the form of a:-

- Direct request: "May I have cigarette?"
- Indirect request: "I would feel better if I had a cigarette".
- Bargain: "I promise I'll not suicide if you give me a cigarette".
- Threat: "If you don't give me a cigarette I'll suicide".
- A plea: "Oh please, please give me cigarette".

Evaluate each request by a suicidal person on its merit or danger. Try not to say "No" to demands, say "Yes", but introduce lots and lots of difficulties with meeting the demand or request. Involve the suicidal person in solving their own demands. Use the demands to 'buy' time and validate their trust in your ability to help. Remember; give honest and factual evidence of your commitment to progress their demand or not

HOW DO WE PREVENT INTERFERENCE DURING THE NEGOTIATION?

Gary was very stern when he explained the following. Don't allow spouses, relatives, friends or workmates to negotiate with a person threatening suicide. They usually exaggerate or trivialise the issues raised. These people may become aroused emotionally and threaten, insult, ridicule or dump guilt and shame on the suicidal person. This will have a negative impact on the success chances of a safe retrieval. It will emotionally arouse the suicidal person.

Anger, frustration, fear, yelling and arguments between them may result. On some occasions, people have been known to complete their suicide after being upset by such encounters. Tell the suicidal person that contact with these people may be made with professional supervision after their retrieval.

WHAT IS MEANT BY 'IF' or 'WHEN'?

When negotiating with a suicidal person, never say "if" always say, "when". "**When** you come back from the edge, I'll have someone waiting to help." Not, "If you come back from the edge, I'll have someone waiting to help." Be careful with what you promise and the timeframe you promise to deliver it. Don't commit to things you can't deliver. Use delay tactics and buy time.

Another good strategy is to ask the suicidal person, "What would I or someone else have to do to stop your suicide?" This involves the suicidal person in their own retrieval solutions. They express their needs and wants allowing us to evaluate a way to address those issues.

WHAT IS MEANT BY THE FACTS & FEELINGS?

Gary also uses his 'FF' principle − facts and feelings. Acknowledge the suicidal person's facts and feelings in the negotiation conversation. They may say, "I'm sad because my wife left me." The fact is their wife left; the feeling is they're sad. Let the person know you heard the fact, and the way they feel about it as well by reflecting. If the negotiator just acknowledges facts, the person's feelings will be missed or ignored.

Conversely, if the feelings are overemphasised, important facts are missed. Remember depressed people want you to listen to what they say, and feel what they feel. Gary wisely advises not to engage in emotional or factual probing of a suicidal person, especially victims of crime or abuse. It is too traumatic during suicide crisis negotiation to bring up their traumatising past events, and may even raise their emotional arousal to a dangerous level. Save any emotional or factual probing or other in depth therapy for controlled and safer counselling conditions by professionals. Remember there's a safer place and a safer time for counselling.

WHAT ARE SOME OF THE DANGERS?

Before, during and after a negotiation watch for:-

- weapons,
- projectiles
- hazardous materials
- booby traps
- Improvised Explosive Devices (IED)
- chemical devices
- incendiary devices
- homemade suicide apparatus such as electric chairs, firearm racks, Russian roulette devices or toxic gas devices

These can be triggered by trip wires, timing devices, electrical/ electronic initiators, mobile phone or radio frequencies, mechanical initiators or the suicidal person themselves. We can't presume that all weapons or devices are for self harm only. They could be used to harm you or others as well. Remember that suicidal people can become homicidal, and homicidal people can become suicidal. The suicidal person may carry more than one weapon or device. An extensive search of the suicidal person and their surrounding location by police is required after retrieval.

WHAT IS THE 'ACTIVE TALKING' MODEL.
When the suicidal person indicates they are just about to actually suicide, urgently use the negotiation 'active talking model' not the 'active listening model'. Active talking is compassionate, with authority and assertiveness. Gary says that it is a strong and urgent plea for someone's life in a caring, but direct way. Tell the person not to suicide. Give them directions to reverse their actions back to a safe and stable status. Tell them you care and want to give their future a chance. When a person is retrieved, ensure they are kept under close supervision until professional help is obtained. Don't let them wander off.

WHO CARES FOR THE CARER?
Gary says, "Most carers are resilient and are able to help themselves however, from time to time carers need outside

support. Whether you negotiated a suicide crisis successfully or unsuccessfully, ensure you consider ministry, defusing, debriefing, therapy or counselling with a support person or support group to make sure you're okay. Always refer to professional support."

He says that carers should have a support network after trauma, but even better than that, is to have support before they go into caring for people which is just as important. The network is for making sure the carer doesn't get vicariously traumatised themselves, fatigued, complacent or resentful under the load of being that carer. Having people praying for you is essential. In other words Gary says, "Who cares for the carer?"

A wise saying is,
"I'm never down, just up.........or getting up" *(John C. Maxwell).*

Better still, Jesus said, "Come to Me all who are weary and heavy laden and I will give you rest." *(Matthew 11:28)*

For support contact The Salvation Army's Suicide Prevention and Bereavement website:-
www.suicideprevention.salvos.org.au

Contact Gary on garyraym@ozemail.com.au

ABOUT THE AUTHOR
- DAVID R NICHOLAS -

David Nicholas is a Baptist pastor who was born in Bristol, England. David has been published in many newspapers and magazines in Australia, England and the United States where he lived with his family for five years while he obtained a Master's degree in Journalism and a Master of Science in Radio Television. Harper Collins published David's book of Australian stories Musical Wheat in 1997.

David was responsible for the creation of The Millthorpe District Museum. He was also the driving force behind a latch key project— the development of a private school (Inaburra) at Menai, South of Sydney. David has also ministered to churches in America, New South Wales, South Australia and Tasmania. He is married to Judith. They have 3 children Mark, Joanne and Andrew.

OTHER BOOKS BY - DAVID R NICHOLAS -
The Pacemaker
Musical Wheat
Honeymoon Corner
Journeys With God
Wigs
Changing Tides
Decurio (In Process)

For more information or to order please contact
David Nicholas via email ronald.31@bigpond.com

Mum meets dad. They were married within a fortnight of this photo being taken

Mum and dad's wedding. Because mum was pregnant she was not allowed to wear white

Me with my younger brother Neil

From top: The five brothers – from oldest to youngest: Gary, Neil, Kevin, Trevor and Brian; Gary in the Navy Cadets. With myself, holding younger brother Brian, and my mum in the far right; The family together. Gary second from right.

Clockwise from top left: Toy guns turn into real guns as all went on to join the police force, and were all at Granville together; Mum in her Salvation Army uniform. Joining the Salvos was a life-changing moment – for all of us; Graduating from Ambulance Training School. Gary pictured back row, next to the instructor on the right

Ambulance graduation day. Top row, second from the left

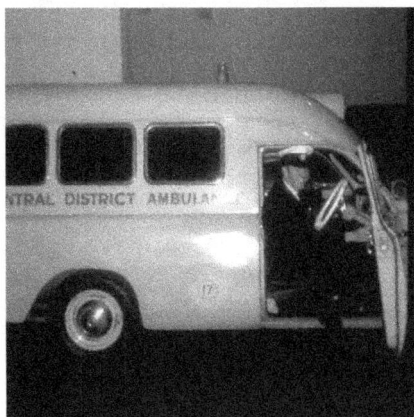

When I first started with the Ambulance

On the job at Marrickville Station in Sydney

Graduating with my good mates from the NSW Police Force. We were all posted to Redfern, Sydney. Gary second from right

As a 23 year-old in uniform at Redfern Station

As a member of the elite Police Rescue Squad

Top: Gary getting ready to descend cliff to rescue a person; Bottom: Resting inside one of the wrecked carriages after completing the rescue. Gary second from left

Gary as a young detective

Three brothers in blue (Gary in the middle)

With wife Michelle in 2004 receiving the NSW Police Medal

In charge as the Duty Officer, overseeing major crime and accident scenes

Gary on patrol

Joining the Salvation Army to help give something back

Receiving the Commissioner's Certificate of Merit for the terrorism risk assessment of the 2003 Rugby World Cup. Pictured with Police Commissioner Ken Moroney AO APM